# *Forgiven*

**Pastor Mark Spitsbergen**

Forgiven
By Dr. Mark Spitsbergen, ThD, MS
Copyright © 2026 by Abiding Place Ministries, San Diego, CA.

ISBN: 979-8-9944098-2-4

Address correspondence to:

Mark Spitsbergen
Abiding Place Ministries
2155 N Campo Truck Trail, Campo CA 91906
www.AbidingPlace.org
AwakeSD@me.com

All rights reserved.

# Table of Contents

Introduction ................................................................. 7

The Rejection ............................................................ 11

The Betrayal ............................................................. 19

The New Beginning .................................................. 24

Repentance Begins .................................................. 27

God Provides an Altar for Forgiveness ..................... 35

Repentance, A New Kind of Life ............................. 44

The Power of the New Life ..................................... 52

The Power of the Transformation of Action ........... 59

The Awfulness of Sin ............................................... 86

Unlimited Forgiveness ............................................. 99

This Covenant Has No Fault ................................. 103

Forgiven ................................................................. 108

Appendix ............................................................... 119

# Introduction

When your life has been full of bad decisions, disappointments, broken relationships, and failures, the greatest thing would be the ability to erase it and start over. While there is no ability to reverse time, there is the ability to be forgiven and have a new start. The whole problem is that the heart of mankind is bound by sin. Sin destroys peoples' lives and relationships. It is the destruction of everything that is good. It is a thief that steals those things most precious to us. It kills everything that we had hoped would live and damns the soul to an eternity without God. Sin is a tyrant that rules without mercy and demands complete obedience of all those under its power.

God created man and endowed him with the ability to walk in the splendor and majesty of His life. God gave man a choice and in the foolishness of his own decision he was snared by the trap of deception. Disobedience opened the door to the floodgates of death and hell. Darkness and shame flooded into his heart and took humanity prisoner. Now sin and darkness is bound in the heart of mankind and has become their own worst enemy. The Apostle Paul described it perfectly when he described the life that is bound by this death and sin:

> "For I do not understand my own actions. For I do not do what I want, but I do the very thing I hate. Now if I do what I do not want, I agree with the Law that it is good. So now it is no longer I who do it, but sin that dwells within me. For I know that nothing good dwells in me – that is, in my flesh. For I have the desire to do what is right, but not the ability to carry it out" (Romans 7:15–18).

People struggle to find their own solution, but there is no remedy to be found. Religions of every kind claim to have the answers, but they all fail to solve the problem. Medical science and psychologists seek for the answers to bring peace to the human heart, but to no avail. There is nothing short of a divine intervention that can change the heart and the human condition.

God, Who passionately loves all humanity, was willing to do whatever it took to rescue mankind from their sinful condition. Even though all that humanity has done is show Him disdain and contempt, even refusing to acknowledge His existence, still He remains unchanged in His love for all the world. His love has come to rescue all mankind and give a brand new beginning to everyone who desires it.

We will walk you through the goodness of God and the events in the history of mankind that help you understand why things are like they are today. Through the story of humanity, it is our desire that you come to understand the love and mercy of God that has granted to all humanity: the opportunity to repent and be forgiven. You will see that the very definition of repent is to have a change of life through the mercy and forgiveness of God. You will discover the goodness of God that is expressed in His mercy, grace, longsuffering, and abundant lovingkindness and truth. In His unfailing love, He has provided a means by which we can be forgiven over and over again if we are willing to turn from our wrongdoing and learn His ways.

This book is about forgiveness. Everyone needs forgiveness, but there really is only one way to be forgiven that matters the most: by the gift of repentance that God has provided for us. He has supplied to us a repentance unto life through the blood of His only begotten Son. This is a brand new beginning with the power to live the life that pleases God. Repentance wipes the slate of our life clean and provides the most amazing wonder of all: oneness with God. Because of God's great love and mercy, He never witholds from us the ability to be forgiven. If we violate this new life in Christ Jesus He continues to give us the ability to recognize the evil that sin is and turn from it.

God in His love and mercy has provided for us a means by which we can be delivered from the snare of sin as many times as we need.

Repentance is a cardinal doctrine of Scripture and its impact is so important that we can't afford to get it wrong. The opportunity to repent is the difference between life and death, Heaven and Hell. God has not left us without a clear description of repentance but has given us hundreds of examples. Yet even more, He has put the Spirit of His Son in our hearts. The Spirit of the Son always desires to please the Father, and once a person has entered into this fellowship of love, they will most certainly know when there has been a violation. If somehow we fail to realize that we have done wrong and need to repent, God's Word and the ministry of the Holy Spirit will make it known.

# Chapter 1
## *The Rejection*

There is a view of God that many have missed. He is the One Who is the most loving and gentle above all who exist. His nature is so pure and lowly that it's hard for humanity to imagine. The pride and selfishness of this world does not exist with Him. The thoughts of evil and corruption are far from Him. In His goodness, He determined to bring forth His own children created in His own image, shaped from the earth – those who He could pour out all of His affections and delights upon.

God went about creating a beautiful home for His children to live in. This home would have the beauty of the stars and the moon at night to shine light upon them, and the beauty of a bright blue sky beaming with the light of the sun to give them light and warmth by day. To make things perfectly complete, He planted the most beautiful garden for them to live in. It was a paradise that was more beautiful and wonderful than anything He had ever made. He filled it with every tree to bring forth fruit and every kind of food that would grow of itself to provide food for His children. There was every kind of flower imaginable to beautify this amazing home and every good and living thing to fill it with an abundance of life and love. There was nothing left out – everything was perfect, and no expense was spared to make this the most beautiful home that God alone could create.

The day had finally arrived for His child to be formed. He came moving to the beauty and splendor of the day that He had created and stepped into the garden. There He knelt down and began to form His child from the fruitful ground that He created. He shaped every part after His own likeness: eyes to see the beauty of life, ears to hear the sound of all living things, and a nose to smell all the wonderful things that grew from the fine dust of the earth. He gave the man hands to feel all that was around him and feet to carry him to all of the places that his Father had created for his dominion. He gave him the ability to take into his mouth all that was good for food so that he might taste all the pleasant things that were made for his enjoyment. God breathed His own Spirit and life into this one who He had formed from the earth. When His Spirit came into His child, all of His nature entered into him. He had the Fathers love for life and purity and His care and gentleness toward all living things.

His Father named him Adam – one made from the earth in the image and likeness of God. God made an abundance of living creatures and brought them to him so that they could meet the one who God would assign to care for them. Adam was assigned by God to give names to all the living creatures that He had made. The place that God had made for him to live was perfect, and the abundance of life in this newly-formed kingdom was filled with wonders to last for eternity. There was only one thing lacking. It was something that went beyond what his Father possessed: God gave Adam a counterpart, a woman. God would bring her into existence in such a way that their lives would be bound together in the oneness of nature and life. They would forever be one, and from this oneness, Adam would also share in God's ability to create after his own image and likeness. God caused a deep sleep to fall upon Adam and He cut open his side. From his own flesh and blood that flowed out of his body, God built the woman from his rib.

Everything was perfect!

It was beautiful, and the day was teeming with the life and abundance that God had created for His children. All that existed was the love of God. Adam would learn the ecstasy and glory of love in his oneness with the woman who was called Chava (Eve). She would be the mother of all humanity. Adam would also learn to love His Father Who had made all of these things for him and gave to him His own life. Together they would be taught how to care for and protect the life that was given to them and all that

Adam had been put in charge of. They would learn to trust their Father and honor Him so that they might learn His eternal knowledge and wisdom.

The first lesson of eternal wisdom that they would learn would be to obey and honor His insights and decrees. God set before His children life and death and gave them the ability to choose to stay with Him and live out the life that He had made for them or to go their own way. So He set in the midst of the paradise that He had made for them a choice: they could freely partake of the fruit of life, or they could choose the fruit of the knowledge of good and evil, knowing that such knowledge was forbidden and would result in their death.

Death!

What an unimaginable concept in the midst of the abundance of life where no death existed or could be fathomed.

It would be impossible for anything to have been more perfect than the beauty of living in paradise with the woman that God had made as flesh of his flesh and bone of his bone. There was nothing but life and love, and the thought of anything else did not exist. Yet one day, toward the evening time, Adam and Eve were walking through the garden. As they walked along, she was drawn toward the tree that bore the fruit that God had warned would cause death.

It was certainly an unfamiliar voice and feeling that called out to her. The voice began to question the motives of her Father. Seeds of doubt and uncertainty were being sown upon the pure soil of her heart. Could her Father really be trusted? Was He really telling her the truth? Was His plan and purpose for her life really what she wanted? The voice cried out, "There is more for you than what you have! Look at how beautiful and desirable this fruit is, and what it will bring to you will be that which you are missing." The voice was relentless. She tried to draw back and proclaim the words of her Father, but each time the alluring desire to discover something far better and more wonderful than she had known pulled her closer. She knew that this was a rejection of the wisdom that she had been taught – and even more, a rejection of her Father – but she became convinced that she was making the right decision.

All this time, Adam remained silent. The one who was given the charge to protect and have dominion seemed too paralyzed to do anything. What his pure and innocent mind could have been thinking at the time is beyond knowing. He could see the response of his beloved wife reaching out to take the fruit that the Father said would result in death, but he did not move. After all, if it would impart to him all the wisdom and knowledge that the Father had, what could be so wrong with that!?

The next morning, Father came to see His children, to spend time helping them discover all the wonders of the life that He had given them. He called out as He was walking through the garden, "Adam, where are you!?" When His children heard His voice, they ran away from Him and hid. Now it was no longer the loving tender voice of their Father that they heard. It sounded different to their disobedient ears. Although it was the same voice that they had always heard, it now caused them fear and terror. Suddenly, they felt differently in His presence and did not want to be near Him. What He wanted for their lives was no longer what they wanted. The limitations and restrictions that He had put on them had been removed, and they were going a different way now. All Adam could say was, "We have hid ourselves from You because we are afraid of You! We thought to hide our shame and nakedness and go on as though all things were the same, but at the sound of Your voice, we knew we could not hide what we had done." The whole of the love, the oneness, and the beauty was gone. There was no smoothing it over and trying to be okay with the wrongdoing. Death and sin was now upon them; they were different from their Father. The Living One now seemed unapproachable by Adam and Eve, who were spiritually dead and belonged to the realm of death. There was no getting around the pain and the shame of it all. They wondered, "Is there any place to hide, so we don't have to feel this way and face Him?"

Relationship was lost. There was no going back. Adam blamed his wife. His wife blamed the serpent. There was no way to say, "I'm sorry." There was no way to say, "Forgive me." There was no way to undo the past and make up for the disobedience. The death and sin that now possessed their natures rejected their Father. They rejected His presence and His discipline. They refused to see that it was their fault – someone else was to be blamed and they refused to be responsible. In fact, the responsibility was in their Father. All that could come out of Adam's mouth was accusation: "It was the woman that You gave me. It was really Your fault, Father, that I am in this situation."

Their rejection of the Father resulted in them having to leave the place that He had made for them to live. It was for their own good. Their disobedience and rejection of Him resulted in them both being possessed and ruled by disobedience. They and their children would not grow more obedient, but would continue to reject and defy their Father. They would take advantage of every good thing and defile it in their own evil natures. So they had to be removed, otherwise they would take the fruit of life and live forever in their state of wickedness.

Yet, in God's compassion and mercy, He promised that He would make a way for them to return. He would bring forth the means of forgiveness through the Seed of the woman who had rejected Him. Her Seed would destroy all that she had destroyed through her disobedience. So God made a sacrifice and provided them with clothing made from skins, and He sent them on their way with a promise of redemption.

# Chapter 2
## *The Betrayal*

God placed cherubims – the ones who protect His presence and guards His glory – to guard the way back into the garden. He knew that the spirit of sin and death that now ruled the nature of His children would defy Him in every way that it could. Their rejection of God could result in nothing less than a separation of relationship. The voice that was once so clear and lovely could no longer be heard. The beauty of His rest and peace was no longer felt. The comfort of His love was absent, and they would have to learn about the realm that they had chosen to live in: one of anguish and toil – the realm of death and betrayal.

Adam and Eve began to have children, children who would never have the privilege of living in the paradise of God on Earth. Although they had rejected the ways of God, His commitment to them would remain. He would extend the knowledge of His redemption to them, which would be testified of by the offerings of their second son,

Abel. The worship of God would cost him his life, and he would ultimately become the first martyr in the Bible.

The rejection of God would find its ultimate betrayal in Cain. Cain, the first son of Adam and Eve, made in their image and likeness, would display the nature of sin and death on a scale that surely was unimaginable. The wisdom and life of God that they were promised by the voice of Satan would begin to manifest in such envy and hatred that Cain rose up against his brother and murdered him. The righteousness of God – which is a way of expressing the sum of all God's actions – would be so despised that Cain would demonstrate the hatred in the heart of man for the ways of God. Once again, man would not seek God's forgiveness for his wrongdoing, but would plead for mercy and protection. The unfathomable mercies of God responded to Cain's pleas and God set a mark of protection on Cain so that he would not be killed by those who would eventually find him as the population of humanity increased. Perhaps God had hoped that one day Cain would do as his brother, who he had killed, and return unto him. However, that never happened. Instead, Cain and all those that descended from him only grew more wicked. They were so given over to wickedness that they refused any likeness of God in their lives.

God had given Adam and Eve a son named Seth, and in the midst of the rise of all this wickedness, Seth had a son named Enos who "called on the name of Yehovah"

(Genesis 4:26). One family in all of the Earth held to God and to His promise. From Enos arose yet another righteous man who cried out to the people, warning them of the judgment of God against sin. His name was Enoch. Enoch was seven generations removed from Adam. Enoch was the man of faith who walked with God. He was so pleasing to God that God translated him into Heaven. However, before Yehovah took him into Heaven, he was God's spokesman on Earth. One of the sermons that he preached is recorded in the New Testament,

> "Behold, the Lord comes with ten thousands of His saints to execute judgment upon all and to convince all that are ungodly among them of all their ungodly deeds that they have ungodly committed and of all their hard sayings that ungodly sinners have spoken against Him" (Jude 1:14–15).

This is a prophecy that still has not been fulfilled, but will be fulfilled at the second coming of Christ Jesus. God is long-suffering and merciful, but when sin –which is disobedience against God and the refusal of God's ways – reaches a certain point, it will be done away with. Ultimately, the wicked will not be able to become more wicked and the wickedest man who has ever lived will rise up to lead men. Men will so want to completely do away with God they will come to fight against the One Who has condemned their sin.

It only took ten generations for man to become so wicked that it was beyond all that could be salvaged. It came to the point that the whole Earth was so filled with wickedness and violence that there was only one righteous man left: Noah. Just think of it, of the hundreds of millions alive on the Earth, there was only one righteous man! Mankind wanted nothing to do with God. At every opportunity to choose good or evil, they chose evil. At every opportunity to accept or reject the ways of God, they rejected Him, and it grieved the heart of God. Men had turned His glory into shame, His goodness into wickedness, and had altogether refused His life. Every blessing of God and act of His mercy was responded to with greater rebellion and disobedience to the point that God repented that He had made man.

It was with God that the concept of repentance was first presented in Scripture. Mankind had become so unlike Him – so destructive and evil – that He repented that He had made man. He turned away from His mercy and determined that those who He had desired to live forever would now die. They had so corrupted themselves that the imaginations of their hearts were continually wicked. There was nothing left to work with. Yet, there was still one man left who held fast to the ways of God. Surely, if God did not act, there would be no one left. In

His mercy, He prepared a way for the one righteous man and his family to be preserved. It would be a new beginning for mankind and an opportunity to start over. He could not wash away the dominion of sin and death, but He could wash away those who were beyond all hope, who refused to have anything to do with His life and His ways.

# Chapter 3

# *The New Beginning*

Because of Noah's righteousness and the mercy of God, his whole household was saved. Of the three sons of Noah, there was one who appears to be devoted to God and His ways – his name was Shem. The Scripture records this by identifying only Shem as being one who served God by saying, "Blessed be Yehovah, the God of Shem." (Genesis 9:26). What is very clear is that men began to corrupt themselves and turn away from any recognition of God. There was only one family that ha d any similitude of desiring t o serve God and walk in His ways: some of the descendants of Shem.

God had never stopped calling out to men. Just as He had called out to Adam in the garden on the day that Adam ran from God and hid himself from His presence, God called out to a man named Abram and Abram responded. It would be in Abram, who would come to be called Abraham, that God would have a family in the Earth who would serve Him. God, the Father of all mankind, would now identify the Seed Who would bring forth the promise made to Eve. God made a promise to the woman who had messed everything up. The woman who stood before God in her rebellion and shame with no indication of repentance received a promise on behalf of all her descendants: one day, through her Seed, redemption would come to all mankind. God would bring forth the ultimate expression of repentance by creating anew all those who would put their trust in the Redeemer.

God promised Abraham a son. Abraham, believing the promise of God, separated Himself unto God and stood apart from all humanity, and God called him a Hebrew. The promised son came by way of a miracle that only God could work, and Sarah gave birth to Isaac. God would work to separate this family unto Himself. The son of Isaac, Jacob, would have twelve sons – and from those twelve sons, a great family would arise. Jacob and his sons went down into Egypt. God, there in the fiery furnace of affliction, would bring forth a family through which He would show His salvation to the human race. In Egypt, the descendants of Abraham would cry out to God in the midst of their affliction and God would come and save them. Their cries for deliverance would not fall on deaf ears, for God had made a promise.

God stepped in and began to reveal to His family that which had not been known about Him since the days of Adam. God would make a distinction between His family and all the families of the Earth. He would show the power of the blood of redemption that Abel trusted in. The power of redemption through the blood would protect the firstborn of Israel when God's judgment fell on the Egyptians. He would bring forth a family out of Egypt and show all the Earth that He alone was God. He revealed His power, His glory, and His holiness. He gave the family of Seth, who was God's replacement for Abel, the revelation of Who He was and they responded to Him as God and King. He gave them laws and commandments so that they would be set apart from all the wickedness of mankind.

Through this family, He would bring forth the Seed Who was promised – the One through Whom God would grant the gift of repentance unto life; the One through Whom man could be made anew spiritually and return to the image and likeness of God, in righteousness and true holiness. Through the blood of the Redeemer, God would grant repentance unto life – a repentance that would bring forth a new creation. The miracle of the promised Seed would crush the power of sin and death, and a new thing would begin: a new life in God.

# Chapter 4
## *Repentance Begins*

Until a person becomes aware of what God has purposed for their lives, they cannot really comprehend sin and wickedness. Until there is an understanding of sin and just how horrible it really is, then there cannot be any real understanding of repentance. We begin to understand repentance in the context of the holiness of God revealed. Of all mankind, only Adam really knew of this great divide, for he alone had been in the presence of God in the fullness of His purity. Now God would begin to make it known to the children of Abraham. God brought His family of about three million people out into the wilderness to separate them from all the other families of the Earth. There, by their willingness to be separated unto Him, He made them a holy and consecrated people unto Himself. He revealed Who He was on the Mountain of Sinai and invited them into His covenant. It was His great desire to dwell in the midst of those made holy to be His children. There they pledged to turn from all the wickedness of the world and to keep His laws and commandments. Yet, they rejected Him once again and all but a few refused to obey. Yet, in His goodness He was willing to remain for the sake of the remnant and moved His dwelling outside their camp. Their interaction with God and His continual mercy and forgiveness is captured in Psalm 107:

> "Because they rebelled against the words of God, and despised the counsel of the Most High. Therefore He bowed down their heart with toil, they stumbled, and there was none to help. They cried unto Yehovah in their trouble, and He saved them out of their distresses. He brought them out of darkness and the shadow of death, and broke their bands in pieces. Let them give thanks unto Yehovah for His mercy, and for His wonderful works to the children of men!
>
> For He has broken the gates of brass, and cut the bars of iron in pieces. Fools because of the way of their transgression, are afflicted because of their iniquities. Their souls loathed any kind of food, until they touched the gates of death. They cried unto Yehovah in their distress, and He saved them; He sent His word, and healed them, and delivered them from their graves. Give thanks unto Yehovah for His lovingkindness, and for His wonderful works to the children of men!" (Ps. 107:11–21).

One of the words used to express repentance is repeated throughout this Psalm, "they cried." The Hebrew word for "crying out" is זָעַק ('zāʿaq'). This word is found in the phrase "and they cried out to the Lord" four times in this Psalm (107:6, 13, 19, 28). They cried to the Lord because He gave them over to the wages of their sin. They had to learn that sin would only result in the same curse of death and separation for Him that had fallen on their first parents, Adam and Eve. They had to learn that God had not changed. He was not going to have fellowship with the unfruitful works of darkness. In the midst of their trouble, they would cry out to God in repentance – and in His mercy that endures forever, He would deliver them. He would show His love and protection to them with mighty signs and wonders, yet they were bent on iniquity and would soon turn away from Him to pursue their iniquity. Yet, every time they would "cry out," or repent, and call upon His name, He would faithfully deliver them.

There are a number of Hebrew words that are used to express repentance. The ones that most often occur are:

נחם, ('naḥum') – to sigh, to breathe strongly, to be sorry, to regret, to groan or to be grieved[1];

שׁוּב, ('shuv') – to turn back[2].

---

[1] (Genesis 6:6, Exodus 13:17, Job 42:6, Jonah 3:10)
[2] (1 Kings 8:47, Ezekiel 14:6, Jonah 3:8,10)

It was God Who first demonstrated the meaning of נחם ('naḥum'), which is to be sorry, to regret, to groan or to be grieved. This expression of repentance occurs 108 times in the Old Testament and allows us to capture the breadth of its meaning. To repent starts with the recognition of wrongdoing. Most importantly, it's wrongdoing that is defined in the context of sin and transgression against the ways of God. Whereas repentance is primarily understood in the context of the action of God's people, it is also used of those who were not His people.

One of the great examples of the usage of both words for repent is witnessed at Nineveh. Their wickedness before the Lord had become so great that God had purposed to destroy them. However, unlike Sodom and Gomorrah, which had gone beyond all redemption, there was still hope for the people of Nineveh. So God sent His prophet, Jonah, to them, and at the preaching of God's judgment upon them, they repented. There was no promise given to them of an opportunity to repent, but still they did repent. The people of Nineveh turned away שׁוּב, ('shuv') from their wickedness. As a result, God regretted/repented (נחם, 'nahum') that He had purposed to destroy them. The proclamation went forth from the King saying,

"Let neither man nor beast, herd or flock, taste anything. Let them not feed, nor drink water, but let man and beast be covered with sackcloth and cry mightily (קרא, 'qara') to God. Yes, let them turn (שוב, 'shuv') everyone from his evil way and from the violence that is in their hands. Who can tell if God will turn (שוב, 'shuv') and repent (נחם, 'nahum'), and turn away (שוב, 'shuv') from His fierce anger that we perish not?" And God saw their works, that they turned (שוב, 'shuv') from their evil way, and God repented (נחם, 'nahum') of the harm that He had said that He would do unto them, and He did it not. (Jonah 3:7-10).

Also in this instance, we see another word similar to זָעַק ('zā'aq') mentioned before that expresses the act of repentance. This time a more common Hebrew word is used for crying out to God or calling to Him: קרא ('qara'). These are expressions of repentance, so we can perhaps understand the earnestness – the cry – that is behind the heart and emotions of those expressing regret, remorse, groaning, and the godly sorrow that exists in repentance. These are the cries of deep sorrow for violating God and the life that He created. The desperation of repentance has an expression that is radically underscored in the Old Testament. As in this story of

Nineveh, repentance is always accompanied by turning away from the wrongdoing.

King David's repentance is one of the iconic acts of repentance that God chose to use as a model to teach us about repentance. David had committed adultery with a woman named Bathsheba. He then killed her husband and married her. King David chose to ignore his wrongdoing and refused to acknowledge his sin. The Spirit of the Lord, Who was given to him, was ignored, and so God stepped in and sent His prophet to deliver His word. When the prophet described the evil deeds of a person used to represent what David had done, David was able to see his wrongdoing from a different perspective and judged that such a one should be killed. When David realized that the prophet was referring to what He had done, he collapsed under the weight of His sin and acknowledged his sin. His repentance was captured in a Psalm that he wrote:

> "To the chief Musician. A Psalm of David. When Nathan the prophet came to him after he had gone into Bathsheba.
>
> "Be gracious unto me, O God, according to Your mercy. According to the multitude of Your compassions, blot out my transgressions. Wash me thoroughly from my iniquity, and cleanse me from my sin. For I know my transgressions, and my sin is

ever before me. Against You, You only, have I sinned, and done that which is evil in Your sight, that You may be justified when You speak, and be in the right when You judge. Behold, I was brought forth in iniquity, and in sin did my mother conceive me. Behold, You desire truth in the inward parts. Therefore, make me know wisdom in my inmost heart. Purge me with hyssop, and I shall be clean. Wash me, and I shall be whiter than snow. Make me to hear joy and gladness, that the bones which You have crushed may rejoice. Hide Your face from my sins, and blot out all my iniquities. Create in me a clean heart, O God, and renew a steadfast spirit within me. Cast me not away from Your presence, and take not Your Holy Spirit from me. Restore to me the joy of Your salvation, and let a willing spirit uphold me." (Psalm 51:1-12)

David was one of the many who were willing to walk with God among God's family. Yet, he had a great moment of failure, a time in his life where he fell into the trap of his own lust. One sin led to another until he found himself so buried in a series of wrong decisions that he could not face the truth. Among other things, he was now an adulterer and a murderer. Still there was the amazing love and goodness of God extended to him. God showed lovingkindness to him as a loving father would. However, he had to acknowledge his sins and turn from them. When the word of God came to him by the prophet, suddenly he was quickened with the reality of his sin and recognized that he had sinned against God alone and done evil in his sight. He had so justified himself that he had become insensitive to the Spirit of the Lord that he had been blessed with. His call for God's mercy and lovingkindness was heard, and when he acknowledged his sin, God forgave him. The prophet Nathan said, "God has put away your sin, and you shall not die" (2 Samuel 12:13). The Lord did not take away His Holy Spirit from him. His heart that was broken and contrite before the Lord longed for the presence of the Lord and the joy of His salvation.

# Chapter 5

# *God Provides an Altar for Forgiveness*

Abel held on to the desire to interact with God. That interaction was depicted around an altar of worship where Abel took the firstborn of the flock and brought them to the Lord. He placed the firstborn upon the altar, and by faith in the coming Redeemer, worshiped God[3]. It would be the coming Redeemer, the Seed promised to his mother, through Whom he would be allowed to return to the paradise of relationship that was lost to his parents. The descendants of Seth, who God had given to replace Abel, carried on with this worship, which is witnessed in the life of Enos, Enoch and Noah. The altar of worship was later observed in the life of Abraham and his sons. When God had established a family in the Earth and brought them into the covenant of relationship with Himself at Sinai, He made known to them everything that must be

---

[3](Genesis 4:4, Hebrews 11:4, 12:24)

done upon the altar of worship to atone for their sins so that He could dwell among them[4].

God loves His children, but how can He have a relationship with them if they continue in their sins? How can there be a relationship unless they will agree to walk with Him? With the power of sin and death bound in their heart, God would by necessity have to provide a means to wipe away the power of sin that ruled them. It would take the coming seed to destroy the power of sin so God would provide a remedy for all those who looked for the Redeemer. To deal with their sins, the worshipper would have to be willing to recognize their sins and turn from them, and God would provide the forgiveness. God made a way to deal with their sins, but it would be absolutely necessary for them to recognize their wrongdoing. One of the reasons for the Law was to help those who were so distant from God to be able to recognize sin and the terrible act of violation that it was against God. This Law was given so that sin might be observed to be exceedingly sinful. Although God held men responsible for their sins before He gave the Law, they were not fully aware of how great a spiritual violation against God their sins really were[5]. So it was the Law that showed them more perfectly the wickedness of sin and the immensity of its treachery against God and His life[6].

---

[4] (Exodus 25:8, 29:36-45)
[5] (Romans 7:13, 1 John 3:4)
[6] (Deut. 28:15-68)

God made a way for all of Israel to repent for their sins so that they could be forgiven of their iniquity. God had made it clear that He would not remain in their midst if they continued in their sin. He underscored that they would only find cursing and death if they were bent on walking in their sins. Just as the Lord had done for Adam and Eve, He set before them life and death, good and evil, blessing and cursing. It was up to each one to choose what they would do. In order to maintain a relationship with them, God gave them a place to meet with Him so that their sins could be atoned for. They would come to understand that if they sinned, one that was innocent must die in their place. They would need to recognize that the cost for their sins was death. To atone for their sins, it would take the blood of an intercessor applied to the altar of God. Once again, the acknowledgment of the sin and the awful consequence would be dramatically displayed in the sacrifice for sin.

How exceedingly awful sin was would be repeated over and over again every time anyone sinned[7]. The lesson they would learn about repenting for their sins was that an innocent one would have to die in their place so that their sins could be pardoned. The person who was repenting for their sins would lay their hands on the innocent offering and confess their sins. Once their sins were confessed, and by confession was laid upon the offering for sin, then the

---

[7] (Lev. 4:1- 7:21)

offering and their sin would be destroyed. The blood of the offering would have the power to atone for their sins so fellowship with God might be restored. The blood would be placed upon the altar, and then the offering would be burned and completely destroyed – the act of rejecting, removing, and destroying the sin that would otherwise result in their removal from His presence. The high priest would execute the sin offering once a year for the nation, but each individual would bring their offering any time they sinned[8].

From the beginning, God had provided an altar where men could come and meet with God. The altar was the place of worship from Abel unto Noah. Later, through the covenant that God made with Abraham, it became established for all Israel at Sinai. It was upon the altar that sin was destroyed and forgiveness was provided. It was upon the same altar that worship and fellowship with God would take place. It was upon the altar that the continual offering of worship would ascend before God, being offered every morning and evening.

There would also be a special day of national repentance that would take place. The day was called the Day of Atonement, which was a day of purification for the people of God. The day of wiping away the old to start a new beginning. God would deal with the national sins of the people of Israel in a single day so that His presence

---

[8] (Lev 16:1-34)

would be able to remain with them. The day began with an offering for sin to purify the high priest so that he could go into an even deeper realm of interaction with God. He would confess His sins while laying his hand upon the sin-offering. It was only at this time that the blood would be actually brought into the Holy of Holies, the place where God's presence dwelt. When the high priest would come into the Holy of Holies, he would see the depictions of the cherub that was placed in the garden to prevent man from returning to the paradise of fellowship with God that they had when sin did not exist. He would walk into the place where the cherubim had their wings stretched out over the mercy seat, the place of God's presence. This was yet another reminder that they had lost the place of fellowship and union that they once had and were still under the judgment of God because of Adam's sin[9]. It was God's desire to put away sin from the midst of His people, but they would have to participate with the blood-offering, the sacrifice for sin.

God demanded that sin be recognized for what it was and renounced. He demanded that sin be destroyed and put out of their midst. He demonstrated over and again that sin would produce death. Their sin would have the same consequence that it had for their ancestors, Adam and Eve. "If they covered their sins, they would not prosper. But if they would confess their sins and forsake

---

[9] (Lev. 16:15-16, Heb. 9:7-8)

them, they would have mercy" (Proverbs 28:13). Below is a brief list of the confession that God required so that sin might be forgiven. God desired that they confess their sins and learn the true consequences of acts of disobedience. The same consequence that fell on Adam and Eve.

> ...<u>confess</u> that in which he has sinned (Lv. 5:5)
> ...and <u>confess</u> over it all the iniquities (Lv. 16:21)
> ...If they <u>confess</u> their iniquity and the (Lv. 26:40)
> ...then he shall <u>confess</u> his sins which he (Nu. 5:7)
> ...if they turn to You again and <u>confess</u> (1 Ki. 8:33)
> ...pray toward this place and <u>confess</u> Your name and turn from their sins (1 Ki. 8:35)
> ...return to You and <u>confess</u> Your name (2 Ch. 6:24)
> ...toward this place and <u>confess</u> Your name (2 Ch. 6:26)
> ...Then I will also <u>confess</u> to you (Jb. 40:14)
> ...<u>confess</u> my transgressions to the LORD (Ps. 32:5)
> ...For I <u>confess</u> my iniquity (Ps. 38:18)
> ...But he who <u>confesses</u> and forsakes them (Pr. 28:13)
> ...and <u>confess</u> the sins of the children of Israel (Ne. 1:6)
> ...and stood and <u>confessed</u> their sins and the (Ne. 9:2)
> ...they <u>confessed</u> and worshiped the LORD (Ne. 9:3)

...to the LORD my God and <u>confessed</u> and said (Da. 9:4)

There were many in the Old Testament that demonstrated their desire to walk with God, and He showed them what was needed. Some were very wicked men and others were righteous. The commonality was that repentance brought the forgiveness that restored their relationship with God.

- Israel's, as a nation[10]
- Ezra's national repentance[11]
- Manasseh's repentance [12]
- Job's repentance[13]

The meaning of repentance reaches beyond what might be conveyed in a single Hebrew or Greek word. The stories relating to repentance provide insight that a single word can not fully convey by itself. In all of these examples, the sins that were committed were acknowledged and put away by the sacrifice of blood. The Lord, in His mercy, then responded, forgave them, and restored them to relationship.

Even when there was such wickedness that it was hard to imagine, God would forgive them if they confessed their sins and poured out the blood of the sacrifice upon

---

[10] (Judg. 10:15–16; 2 Chron. 15:4; Ezra 6:21)
[11] (Ezra 9:1–3, 5–6; Ezra 10:1)
[12] (2 Chron. 33:12–13)
[13] (Job 42:6)

His altar. God's mercy surpassed all their wickedness and evil, like in the case of Manasseh. Manasseh was one of the most, if not the most, wicked of the kings among God's people[14]. It was because of the sins of Manasseh that God ultimately had to bring judgment upon the whole nation[15]. Yet, when Manasseh was carried away to Babylon and placed in prison, he cried out to God, and God forgave him.

> "Therefore the Lord brought upon them the captains of the host of the king of Assyria, who took Manasseh among the thorns, bound him with chains, and carried him to Babylon. And when he was in affliction, he besought the LORD his God and humbled himself greatly before the God of his fathers, and prayed to him. And He responded to him, heard his supplication, and brought him again to Jerusalem into his kingdom. Then Manasseh knew that the LORD he was God" (2 Chronicles 33:11–13).

Although Ahab cannot really be an example of true repentance, still God's great mercy was shown when Ahan humbled himself before the Lord and sought mercy. Ahab and Jezebel led all of Israel into great sin and wickedness. When God announced to Ahab by his servant Elijah that

---

[14] (2 Kings 21:11-17)
[15] (2 Kings 24:3)

His judgement would fall upon him, Ahab tore his clothes, fasted, and laid down in sackcloth. The Lord's merciful and lowly response to Elijah was,

"See how Ahab humbled himself before Me? Because he humbled himself before Me, I will not bring the destruction in his days. But in his son's days will I bring the destruction upon his house" (1 Kings 21:29).

One of the foremost dispositions of repentance before God is captured in a single verse,

"If My people, who are called by My name, shall humble themselves, pray, seek My face, and turn from their wicked ways, then will I hear from Heaven, forgive their sin, and heal their land" (2 Chronicles 7:14).

# Chapter 6

# Repentance, A New Kind of Life

Throughout all the generations of humanity, God has worked to one end: to raise mankind from their spiritual death; to completely forgive and restore them to the former state of glory that they had before they disobeyed; to bring men back to what they were before sin and death took them away. It's been His desire from the very beginning to renew man in His image and likeness, in righteousness and true holiness.

God had made a promise to Eve that He would bring forth a Seed to crush the head of the deceiver who gained dominion over her and Adam and subsequently all of their descendants. Abraham was willing to agree with Father's plan to bring forth the Seed, so God separated him to bring forth the family from whom the Seed would come. Through all of the challenges, sin, acts of treason, and rebellion of Abraham's family, there was always a remnant that remained true to God's plan until the fullness of time came and the Messiah, Christ Jesus, was born of a young virgin named Mary.

Christ Jesus was born of a woman under the Law and was perfect concerning all that God had commanded. Where Adam had failed, Jesus succeeded. He did not allow any of the sinful acts of treason against the Lord to enter into His life. He was found to be the blameless Lamb of God so that all of the sins of humanity could be laid upon Him as it had been on the tens of thousands of offerings that represented Him. He was born in the midst of the same evil-hearted men that had existed since the time of Cain. He was treated with contempt and cruelty until the day that He was hung upon a cross to bear the sins of the whole world. Jesus, through death, destroyed him that had the power of death. The power of sin and death would have no more rights over all who would come to the sacrifice that He had made. He went down into Hell and gained the keys of Hell and death. Through His resurrection, He brought forth resurrection life for all who would receive. He purchased forgiveness of sin and resurrection life for all who would believe. Through Him, the Father has granted to all who will receive, repentance unto life and the forgiveness of sins.

Today, we are commissioned by Christ Jesus to go into all the world and declare repentance and forgiveness to every person[16]. Anyone who will call upon the Lord Jesus will receive this new kind of life. The past will be destroyed – all the sins and iniquities will be put to death and completely washed away through cleansing by the blood and the washing of being born again[17]. The heart and spirit that came under the dominion of sin would be put to death, and a new creation would come forth by the miracle of the new birth for anyone who was willing. This would be a new kind of repentance, a repentance unto life. This repentance would not just cleanse the sins from being held against the offerer, but would take away the power of sin permanently. This new kind of repentance would result in the washing of the water of regeneration and renewing of the Holy Spirit[18]. This would be a forgiveness of sins that would remove the sins of the **past** as far as the east is from the west[19]. With such a radical transformation that only the new birth could bring, every sin of the past would be remembered no more.

The new birth would bring the greatest kind of repentance ever thought of. It would make a person a new creation in which everything old was put to death and everything new would begin. It would be impossible for a sinner to remember all the sins that they had committed. Their lives were not lived like those in Israel, who offered a

---

[16] (Luke 24:47)
[17] (Mt 26:27; John 3:3-6; Titus 3:5)
[18] (Titus 3:5, John 3:3-6)
[19] (Rom. 3:25, Psalms 103:12, Isa 38:17)

sin offering every time a sin was committed. The life of those who were of the world was a lifelong continuance of one sin after another. So in one act of God's grace, every sin was removed by the repentance unto life in which a person was given a new inner being, a new spirit and a new heart. The old person was crucified – destroyed – just as the sin offering was destroyed at the altar under the Law[20]. Through this miracle salvation, a new person was raised up with Christ Jesus. Newly formed, not from the fine dust of the Earth, but in Christ Jesus. Old things all passed away in a miraculous instant and everything became new[21].

God has now granted to everyone "repentance unto life" (Acts 11:18). Still, it is a repentance that must be participated with so the miraculous change of life may come. Now it's more than just a change of mind and attitude – more than just a turning away – but it's a radical and supreme repentance that results in a new existence. The one who comes to Jesus is purified, made righteous and holy and given the righteousness of God.

The introduction of the New Covenant begins with the cry to repent, heard in the message of John the Baptizer. The New Covenant cry on the lips of Jesus is: "Repent!" The New Covenant message to repent is the message of conversion. To convert 'ἐπιστρέφω' ('epistrepho'), which

---

[20] (Lev. 3:1-7:15)
[21] (2 Cor. 5:17, Rom. 6:4, 6, Col. 2:11-13)

like its Hebrew counterpart שוב ('shuv'), is to turn back or even turn around[22]. It's God's call to come to the altar where He has made a sacrifice for our sins. It's God's call to start something brand new in the life of anyone who will respond. The call of all His preachers is the same: repent and turn to God and to "do works that show that you have repented" (Acts 26:20). That is to say, "Repent, turn to God, and have the evidence that everything about your life has changed." One of the most important points that is made in both the Old Testament and the New Testament is: through the act of repentance, sin is removed. What could be more crucial? What could be more important to absolutely get right than the knowledge of how the power of sin is removed and every stain of sins committed are wiped away?

The message of repentance spoken by John was to those who were born into the Covenant, yet never realized the life of the Covenant. God warned everyone through John to "repent or perish!" "...the axe is laid to the root and every tree that does not bring forth fruit will be cast into the fire" (Matthew 3:10). Consider the reality that it was God Who was speaking. It was the Judge of all flesh Who spoke through John! Who can justly make the argument that this belongs to a foreign understanding of God? To speak of the God of the Old Testament as being someone different than the God of the New Testament is idolatry.

---

[22] (Acts 3:19, Psalms 19:7; 51:13; John 12:40 etc..)

To somehow believe that God has changed His mind about sin in any way is a tragic mistake – God is unchanging! Good men slip into the error of having a form of godliness, but denying the power of it in so many ways. They will say that our sins have been removed and we have been made righteous, but deny the power to live in that righteousness. God underscored this truth in the transitional message that John the Baptizer preached of "repentance for the remission of sins." John described this new kind of repentance, the change of mind and life that the Messiah would bring, as a far greater baptism of change when he said, "I indeed baptize you with water unto repentance, but He Who comes after me is mightier than I, Whose shoes I am not worthy to bear. He shall baptize you with the Holy Spirit and fire, Whose fan is in His hand, and He will thoroughly purge His floor and gather His wheat into the storehouse – but He will burn up the chaff with unquenchable fire" (Mt. 3:1-12). We know how Jesus felt about the ministry of John, for we observe Christ Jesus submitting to the ministry of John – He was also baptized in this water of repentance. Jesus, who had no sin to repent of, stepped into the immersion into repentance. We should take heed!

There are primarily two words that are used for repentance in the New Testament: μετανοέω ('metanoeo') and μεταμέλομαι ('metamelomai'). 'Metanoeo' is used for repentance more than the other: 38 times. The basic meaning of 'metanoeo' is "to change the mind" or "sorrow for wrongdoing," and what is implied is a consecration to change. Repentance speaks of the means by which sin is erased and the entrance into the new life in Christ Jesus begins.

Repentance is found approximately 110 times from Genesis 6:6 to Revelation 16:1. There are several Hebrew and Greek words that are used for repentance or that implies repentance.

1. נחם, ('nachum') to sigh, to breathe strongly, to be sorry [23]
2. שוב, ('shuv') to turn back[24]
3. μετανοέω ('metanoeo') this noun can be viewed as a change of mind but its equivalence to the Hebrew 'nachum' in the Septuagint speaks of regret and the sorrow over sin[25]. The related verb μετάνοια ('metanoia') is a change of mind and attitude toward sin itself and its cause, not merely the consequences of sin. Both imply the subsequent turning away from sin both in thought and action.[26]
4. μεταμέλομαι ('metamelomai') is more of regret of the consequences of sin, not the cause[27]

---

[23] (Gen. 6:6, Ex. 13:17, Job 42:6, Jonah 3:10)
[24] (1 Ki. 8:47, Ezek. 14:6)
[25] (Lk. 13:3)
[26] (Mt. 3:8, 11, 9:13, Lk. 24:47)
[27] (Mt. 27:3, 2 Cor. 7:8)

5. ἐπιστρέφω/ Στρεφω ('epistrepho'/'etrepho') return, turn back; often used to translate the Hebrew word שׁוּב ('shuv')[28]; also a word used by John for repent[29]
6. ἀμεταμέλητος ('ametameletos') irrevocable[30]

Today God has granted to everyone the opportunity of "repentance unto life." The foundation for which we build our understanding of the meaning of repentance unto life is found in the Old Testament, so it is from the Hebrew words that we come to understand the meaning of the Greek words. The Hebrew equivalent of 'metanoeo' is נחם ('nachum'). The Hebrew word 'nachum' is primarily used of God repenting and is translated by 'metanoeo' in the Septuagint[31]. It is also used with regard to men repenting[32]. Finally, 'metanoeo' is translated several times by the Hebrew word שׁוּב ('shuv'), which means "to return" (Isa. 46:8). **In view of this, we can be certain that repent and repentance are words that are used for more than the initial salvation experience when a person is born again.** It is the mercy of God that is made available to all if we sin. If we sin, we confess our sins, and He is faithful and just to cleanse us from all unrighteousness[33].

---

[28] (Acts 3:19, 15:19, 26:20)
[29] (John 12:40)
[30] (Rom. 11:29, 2 Cor. 7:10)
[31] (Amos 7:3, 6, Joel 2:13, 14, Jonah 3:9-10; 4:2; Zech 8:14; Jer 4:28; 18:8,10)
[32] (Jer. 8:6; 38:19)
[33] (1 John 1:9)

# Chapter 7

# *The Power of the New Life*

When a person comes to Christ Jesus, they come to Him for a transformation of life! We come to be released from our sins by His own blood and born of His Spirit (Rev. 1:5; John 3:3-6). This is a repentance unto a new life altogether! This is a repentance that results in the life of God dwelling within us. This repentance results in the life of sin and death being abolished and the life of God being imparted. Through this repentance, man returns to the life of God lost by Adam. We are transformed from the life of Adam to the life of Jesus Christ. This is the expression of the ultimate change of mind and heart – through the miracle of the new birth, we have received a new spirit and a new heart[34].

---

[34] (Heb. 8:10; 10:16; 2 Cor 3:3; Ezek. 36:26)

God gave us more than just the forgiveness of sins – He removed the body of the sins of the flesh[35]. This is more than a change of mind – this is a regeneration, a transformation of life. Repentance is a divine action of God upon the heart of man, brought about by the working of the Holy Spirit, Who convicts men of their sins and calls men to a new kind of divine life[36]. When a person responds to the Holy Spirit's conviction, God works the miracle of change. The ultimate and final result of this act is forgiveness of sins that results in a new life: the life of God! Repentance is all about turning to a new life in God and turning away from sin; turning to God to live the life that He created Adam to have; turning to Christ Jesus to live His life; turning to the heavenly and the life created anew; turning to walk in the Spirit and be led by the Spirit to live the life of the Holy Spirit.

When we are born again, we are born into the Kingdom of God. We were brought back to a place that is greater in many ways than the one that Adam and Eve lost. Why? Because God has given us the life of Christ, and our existence is found in Him. We are empowered to make Christ Jesus our sovereign King and Lord and submit to His rulership, protection, and keeping power. Salvation repentance renounces the former life and commits to living the life of the Holy Spirit. The work of

---
[35] (Col. 2:11; Rom 6:6)
[36] (2 Pet 2:3-4; Jn 1:12; 4:10,13; 7:38-39; 1 Jn 3:3; Mt 3:11)

salvation purified us and made us a people that are zealous to walk in the ways of God[37]. Having been delivered from the tyranny of sin and Satan, <u>we deny</u> (ἀρνέομαι, 'arneomai') ungodliness and worldly lusts, and live soberly, righteously, and godly, in this present world. Now we have the power and ability to live the kind of life that God intended us to have when He created Adam and Eve. He has put His love and life back in us and we have no desire to have fellowship with the unfruitful works of darkness, but rather <u>reprove</u> (ἐλέγχετε, 'elenchete') them. Both these two words deny (ἀρνέομαι, 'arneomai') and reprove (ἐλέγχετε, 'elenchete') carry with them the meaning of turning away from sin continually.

Jesus came to call sinners to repentance. He emphasized the sinner who smote his breast – asking God to forgive him of his sins – saying he was the one justified [38]. Repentance is correlated to believing the Gospel and recognizing that Jesus alone forgives sins[39]. Jesus preached that repentance was the means by which the people would escape destruction[40]. Repentance is so important to God that all of Heaven rejoices over one sinner who repents[41]. When Jesus sent out His apostles to preach, they were commissioned to preach that every man should repent[42].

---

[37] (Titus 2:14)
[38] (Luke 18:13-14)
[39] (Mark 1:15)
[40] (Luke 13:1-5)
[41] (Luke 15:7, 10)
[42] (Mark 6:12)

That same commission is given to us today, "..that repentance and remission of sins should be preached in His name among all nations, beginning at Jerusalem." (Luke 24:47).[43]

"Repent," was the message that Peter preached at the first New Testament Church meeting on Pentecost. His second recorded sermon was nearly the same when he preached to the crowd saying, "Repent and turn, that your sins may be blotted out" (Acts 3:19). He defines repentance as every person turning from their iniquity [44]. Paul gives an even more specific definition of repentance when he said,

> "...to open their eyes, and to turn them from darkness to light, and from the power of Satan unto God, that they may receive forgiveness of sins, and inheritance among them who are sanctified by faith that is in Me" (Acts 26:18).

Paul's definition of repentance was a radical change of life – with the conduct to prove it – which He equated to faith[45].

The message of repentance is a message of turning to God and turning away from sin. There is probably no one in the four Gospels or in the Epistles who emphasized this more than John. Although men are correct in saying that

---
[43] (Matthew 28:18-19; Mark 16:15-16)
[44] (Acts 3:26)
[45] (Acts 26:20; 20:21)

the exact word for repentance is not used μετανοέω ('metanoeo'), the message of repentance – which is perfectly described by having a change of life, or turning to God – is radically presented by the Apostle John. John describes this radical change as being either of the light or of darkness, of the truth or a lie, of God or of the Devil, of righteousness or sin, of the Spirit or of the world. What terminology could possibly describe the turning to God that repentance brings more perfectly? It is in the Gospel of John that we hear Christ Jesus give the radical commands to, "Go and sin no more" (Jn. 5:14, 8:11). Jesus said that those who follow Him do not walk in darkness, and nothing could more explicitly describe the change that repentance brings[46]. Turning to God is described as not being of this world, even as Jesus is not of this world. Also, there is a distinction between those who are from above and those who are from beneath. He makes it clear: to believe is to obey! He emphasized that the inability of Israel to turn to God was because they were not able to believe the Gospel[47]. If there is no belief, then there is no turning in behavior. Likewise, if there is no turning in behavior, it is evidence of no belief[48]. Similarly, Paul related disobedience to unbelief[49]. What could be a more radical description of the many words that convey the

---

[46] (Jn. 8:12)
[47] (John 12:38-40)
[48] (1 John 1:6; 2:4, 6, 11, 16-17, 29, 3:4, 6,7,8,9,10, 14, 17, 24 etc.)
[49] (Heb. 3-4)

meaning and effects of repentance than to be "born again?" It is in the Gospel of John that salvation is described in terms of being born again[50]. John speaks of the transformed life louder than all others, and nothing can describe repentance and turning to God more completely. "You must be born again," is the strongest way that God has ever called men to repent.

Salvation and repentance scriptures:
- Acts 3:19–20 – Repent ye therefore, and be converted, that your sins may be blotted out, when the times of refreshing shall come from the presence of the Lord;
- Acts 2:38 – Then Peter said unto them, Repent, and be baptized every one of you in the name of Jesus Christ for the remission of sins, and ye shall receive the gift of the Holy Ghost
- Acts 3:19–20 – Repent ye therefore, and be converted, that your sins may be blotted out, when the times of refreshing shall come from the presence of the Lord;
- Acts 5:31 – Him hath God exalted with his right hand to be a Prince and a Saviour, for to give repentance to Israel, and forgiveness of sins
- Acts 26:19–20 – I was not disobedient unto the heavenly vision: But shewed first unto them of

---

[50] (John 3:3-8)

Damascus, and at Jerusalem, and throughout all the coasts of Judaea, and then to the Gentiles, that they should repent and turn to God, and do works meet for repentance .

- Matthew 3:8 – Bring forth therefore fruits meet for repentance

# Chapter 8

# *The Power of the Transformation of Action*

We are made a new creation with a new heart and new spirit. God has put His Holy Spirit in us and the Holy Spirit is also with us. We are baptized in the fire of His Spirit and have His life flowing out of us like rivers. We have been given the strength of the Lord and the power of His might to walk with Him[51]. By His divine power He has given us everything that we need for His life and godliness to rule our lives[52]. The salvation that has been given to us has perfectly equipped us to have power over all of the works of Satan[53]. The righteousness that we have been given in Christ Jesus is at work to develop us in all the ways of God. The holiness that we have been given empowers holiness in all our works. Still we are faced with

---

[51] (Eph 6:10)
[52] (2 Peter 1:3)
[53] (Luke 10:19; Rom 6:41-2; 1 John 2:1; 1 Peter 2:24; 1 John 2:14)

much opposition in a world ruled by the prince and the power of the air, the god of this world[54]. As we grow and learn to follow the Holy Spirit, a provision has been made for us *if* we sin. "*If* we sin, we have an intercessor with God, Jesus Christ the righteous." He is our mercy seat [55]. God made provision through His Son, Christ Jesus, that the same kind of separation that took place when Adam sinned would not have to happen again. Just as those under the Law in the first covenant had a provision to find forgiveness for their sins, God has made provision for sins in the New Covenant. Unlike those under the Old Covenant, there now remains no more sacrifice for sins. Jesus, as the Lamb of God, provided His blood as provision for an everlasting covenant. If we sin, we come with the blood of Jesus, Who cleanses us from all sin. The blood of Jesus is the blood of the New Covenant that was given for the forgiveness of sins[56]. We are promised,

> "If we should confess our sins, He is faithful and righteous to forgive us of the sins and to cleanse us from all unrighteousness" (1 John 1:9).

Repentance is one of the foremost foundational doctrines of the Bible and is among the first principles of the New Testament. The foundational doctrines of the New Testament has at the top of the list <u>repentance</u> from

---

[54] (Eph 2:2)
[55] (1 John 2:1-2, Heb 7:25, Rom 8:34)
[56] (Mt 26:28; Luke 24:47; Acts 10:43; Rom 3:25)

νεκρῶν ἔργων ('nekron ergon,' works of death) καὶ πίστεως ἐπὶ θεόν ('kai pisteos epi theon,' and faith upon God)[57]. We build the entirety of our life in Christ Jesus upon the foundation of repentance of these works of death (sin) and faith in what God has done for us in redemption. Maturity in the life of Jesus will not exist without the foundation. The two most fundamental "head" doctrines of the New Testament are repentance, μετανοίας ('metanoias') and faith, πίστεως ('pisteos'). Paul described this as the Gospel that he preached to both Jews and Gentiles, "repentance to God and faith in our Lord Jesus Christ" (Ac. 20:21). Repentance and faith towards God have been described as "inseparable twins, the one cannot live without the other (Matthew Henry's Commentary). "The church Fathers generally understand dead work as simply sinful works" (Spence-Jones, ed., Hebrews, The Pulpit Commentary 1909, 158.). "It does not mean that listeners are to leave the basics behind, since repentance, faith, and other teachings (Heb 6:1b–2) are presupposed rather than abandoned" (Craig R. Koester, 2008, 303.).

Repentance through faith in the blood of Jesus delivered us from every dimension of sin and death. When Adam and Eve disobeyed God, they died spiritually. At that moment, they came under the power of sin and death. The law of the Spirit of life in Christ Jesus liberated us from the law of sin and death when we were born

---

[57] (Hebrew 6:1)

again [58]. As those alive from the dead, we live in the divine nature[59]. Yet we still have to contend with temptation from the tempter! The assailing influence of the powers of darkness and fleshly lusts war against us[60]. If we should sin after being born again, we need to have the ability to be forgiven of our sins. The act of sin gives death power over our lives[61]. Repentance unto salvation through faith in the blood of Jesus Christ breaks every claim of death[62]. We do not live our lives focused on sin rather we are living out the new life of righteousness in Christ. However if we sin we should be very focused on the cleansing that comes from our Redeemer Who delivers us from the power and claim of sin against our lives. There is no one who has the right to change the definition of repentance! The power of repentance unto salvation, which is ours through faith in the blood of Jesus, releases us from our sin. It is the blood of Jesus that sets us free. It's the blood of Jesus that cleanses from all sin. Repentance through faith in the blood of Jesus delivers us from all the effects of sin and its guilt[63]. Through the mercies of God, none of our identity in Christ Jesus is lost – rather, the enemy of that identity is removed. Through faith in the blood of Jesus, we are completely cleansed and forgiven with no conscience of

---

[58] (Romans 8:2)
[59] (2 Peter 1:4)
[60] (1 Pet. 2:11)
[61] (Rom. 6:16, John 8:34, 2 Peter 2:19; James 1:15)
[62] (1 John 1:9, 2 Cor. 7:9-10, Eph. 1:7; Mt 26:27)
[63] (Rom. 6:16-18, Acts 8:22)

sin or trespass[64]. The blood of Jesus will never lose its power

*If* we sin, God the Holy Spirit produces godly sorrow[65]. This is not condemnation, this is the call of God to come to the altar. Godly sorrow works repentance unto salvation. Repentance (μετάνοια, 'metanoia') is more than just a "change of attitude or feeling," which is communicated through μεταμέλομαι (metamelomai'). Many have changed their attitude about their wrongdoing, but it did not result in their salvation. Judas is an example of a person who just "changed his mind" or had regret (μεταμέλομαι, 'metamelomai'). He regretted that he had betrayed Jesus and he returned the silver, but he did not come to a place of repentance, and he died in his sin[66]. There is a godly sorrow for sin and there is a worldly sorrow. Worldly sorrow has no remedy for the guilt and shame – much less for the sin! However, godly sorrow removes the sin and removes the guilt and shame of sin when it results in repentance[67].

We are given purity, holiness, righteousness, and all that is in the life of Christ Jesus by the Holy Spirit. However, we are still called to cleanse ourselves from the uncleanness of the flesh and spirit, perfecting holiness in

---

[64] (Heb 10:2)
[65] (2 Cor 7:10)
[66] (Matthew 27:3)
[67] (2 Cor 7:10)

the fear of God[68]. We have been purified by the blood of Jesus and are commanded to guard against all impurity. We were perfectly cleansed when we were born again, but we must stand against the iniquity that would attempt to take hold of us and lead us away. We are to put to death any sin that would draw us away[69]. We were made pure and were empowered to remain pure from all the impurity of this world. Once again, our oneness with Christ Jesus and divine empowerment in the Holy Spirit gives us the authority to remain unspotted by the world[70]. But *if* we sin, then sin contaminates us with its uncleanness[71]. The remedy is faith in the cleansing blood of Jesus which is applied to our lives through the forgiveness that God has supplied to us[72].

Only the blood of Jesus can purify us from all the filthiness of sin. In the midst of all the darkness and evil in this world, we stand as the sons of God. We are given the ultimate of all promises: to see God just as He is, because we will be like Him[73]. Yet at the same time, we are exhorted as the children of God to purify ourselves even as He is pure[74]. We were definitely purified when we were

---

[68] (2 Cor. 7:1)
[69] (Rom 8:13; Col 3:5)
[70] (James 1:27; Jude 23)
[71] (Rom. 6:16-19; 2 Cor 7:1)
[72] (James 5:15; Col 1:14; Eph 1:7)
[73] (1 John 3:2)
[74] (1 John 3:3)

born again, but there is a call to keep ourselves pure[75]. This is not a sin-consciousness but a God-consciousness. We have the life of Christ Jesus and if evil rises up we will be grieved by it. We are those who He made pure and holy, who have no desire to be anything less. The work of God's grace in our lives is growing and maturing in all that He has given us. He is our wisdom, our righteousness, our holiness, and our redemption, and we are to remain in Him[76]. Remaining in Him is our holiness and purity. We received the gift of His holiness and righteousness when He came into our lives, but we grow and mature in every dimension of the life that He has given us. Although we are not in the flesh but in the Spirit, still we are called to put to death anything unlike God that would work in our bodies[77].

Christ Jesus is likened to the mercy seat (BHS: כַּפֹּרֶת 'kipporet/ LXX: ἱλαστήριον, 'hilasterion') that was in the Holy of Holies, the place where the blood was applied to wipe away (כפר, kuppar) the sins that the nation of Israel had committed throughout the year[78]. Paul said,

> "Whom God set forth as the mercy seat (ἱλαστήριον, 'hilasterion') through faith in His

---

[75] (Titus 2:14)
[76] (1 Cor 1:30; Jer 23:6; He 10:19)
[77] (Rom 8:9, 13)
[78] (Lev 16:16)

blood, to declare His righteousness for the forgiveness of sins that are **past**…" (Rom. 3:25).

Just as the sins of the past year for the nation of Israel were removed so our sins of the past are whipped away. John also said that Jesus was the mercy seat for our sins and "for the sins of the whole world," and that God loved us and "sent His Son to be the mercy seat for our sins" (1 John 2:2, 4:10). As the mercy seat, Christ Jesus is the place where cleansing from sin is found. As our High Priest, Jesus is the One Who makes intercession for our sins [79]. Certainly this speaks of the ever-available fountain for cleansing if we should sin.

> "But if we walk in the Light as He Himself is in the Light, we have fellowship with one another, and the blood of Jesus Christ, His Son, purifies us from all sin. If we should confess our sins, He is faithful and righteous to forgive us of the sins and to cleanse us from all unrighteousness. …But if anyone sins, we have an Advocate with the Father, Jesus Christ the righteous. And He is the mercy seat for our sins, and not for ours only, but also for the whole world." (1 John 1:7, 9; 2:1-2).

These passages of scripture make one complete picture of the cleansing from sin that is in the blood of Jesus. They

---

[79] (Heb. 2:17, 7:25)

are linked together grammatically and also by context. We have been given the blood of Jesus for all our past sins and if we sin after we have been cleansed His blood is still supplied to cleanse us once again.

The application of the blood upon the altar was not efficacious unless confession of sins was first made. Obviously, all those in Israel understood this perfectly well. It was so repetitious and basic that it was impossible not to be foundational to the first century New Testament saints. If a person sinned, in the Old Testament and in the there had to be a confession of the sins for the application of the blood to be viable to wipe away (כפר, 'kuppar') the sins. What we come to understand is that it is also the same in the New Testament as well. As it was for the examples in the Old Testament so it is now for all in the New Testament. Only now it is by the eternal blood of the covenant given to us by Jesus[80]. There are five verses in the New Testament that directly speak of confession of sins:

- …if we <u>confess</u> our sins… (1 John 1:9)
- …as they <u>confessed</u> their sins… (Mt. 3:6)
- …<u>confess</u> your sins to one another… (Jas. 5:16)
- …All <u>confessed</u> and revealed practices…(Acts 19:18)
- …<u>confessing</u> their sins were baptized… (Mk. 1:5)

There is only one way to make things right in a relationship between any two people. We have to be both

---

[80] (Hebrews 13:20; 9:12)

willing to confess our sins and to hear if someone thinks we have wronged them. There is no way to forgive or be forgiven unless there is a confession of the problem [81]. So it is with our relationship with God. Knowing that if we sin it's against God alone that we sinned and done evil in His sight [82]. "If we should confess our sins, He is faithful and righteous to cleanse us from all unrighteousness." This verse of scripture in 1 John 1:9 is not referring to the power of sin or generic sin, because ἁμαρτίας ('hamartias', sins) is plural. It is by confession then that He with His own blood cleanses us from sin. It would be similar to the person in the Old Covenant who would bring the blood of the sin offering for a cleansing, but instead we come with the blood of Jesus.

> "If we confess (ἐαν ὁμολογωμεν [ean homologōmen]). Third-class condition again with ἐαν [ean] and present active subjunctive of ὁμολογεω [homologeō], 'if we keep on confessing.' Confession of sin to God and to one another (James 5:16) is urged throughout the N. T." (A.T. Robertson, Word Pictures in the New Testament; 1 Jn. 1:9.)

Can there be a deep heartfelt love and yet no sense of sorrow for hurting the person that is loved? Was Peter

---

[81] (Matthew 18:15-17; Luke 17:3-4; Mark 11:25)
[82] (Psalms 51:4)

wrong when, after he faced the reality of his betrayal of Jesus, his repentance was so deep that he wept bitterly? This indeed was an act of grief and repentance for what he had done and certainly a definition of μετανοέω ('metanoeo'). We know that he both sought forgiveness and was forgiven, because he received the restoration that only repentance can bring and was back with the other disciples by Sunday, which was three days later. Jesus told Peter that after he "turned again" (ἐπιστρέφω, 'epistrepho'), which is another word for repent, he was t strengthen the others. "But I have prayed for you that your faith will not fail. And when you return again, strengthen your brothers" (Lk. 22:32). So deep was his remorse that tradition says that whenever Peter heard a rooster crow, he would fall on his knees and weep.

In view of the many scriptures on repentance and the fundamental meaning of repentance, we can be certain that repentance (or repent) is a word that is used beyond the initial salvation experience. If a person sins, both in the Old Testament and in New Testament there must be a confession of the sins for the application of the blood to be viable for the removal of sin. The only exception would be at the time when we become a new creation. There is a complete removal of all sin through the new birth. The confession of sins is the recognition and renouncing of them by the blood of Jesus. The blood of Jesus is the overcoming power that shuts down every claim of sin and empowers us to never commit that sin again.

The Old Testament saints came to the altar and confessed their sins over their offering so that they might be forgiven. Those who were moved by God to come to be baptized by John confessed their sins and were baptized in repentance. The disciples of Jesus also baptized in the same manner [83]. We also observe from James that it was the instruction of the saints to confess their faults one to another and pray over them (James 5:16). So we can be certain that the confession of sins, which is a vocalization of asking for forgiveness, is a cardinal New Testament doctrine. The clear association between forgiving one another and being forgiven by God is established in the Lord's prayer, "forgive us our sins as we forgive..." (Mt. 6:12). There is no place in Scripture that says that sins are automatically forgiven. Rather, the emphasis is given on confession of sins throughout the Bible. The Old Testament examples showed us a continual repetition of the need to confess sins in the act of repentance and renouncing sins. There is nowhere in Scripture that indicates anything different. If this is indeed how God has meant for sins to be cleansed, we cannot afford to make a mistake here. There should be a vocal disdain and renunciation of sins in The New Testament. This does not take away from redemption power in the blood – rather it

---

[83] (John 3:22, 26, 4:1-2)

establishes the efficacy of the blood. This has nothing to do with Law-works, but is faith-works. It would be far better if a person never sinned. But if we sin we don't ignore the sin or behave as though we did nothing wrong – rather, we ask for forgiveness, and God in His mercy forgives us by faith in the blood of Jesus.

The precedence is established: the guilty person must confess his sins[84] – we are to acknowledge our iniquity[85]. Aaron, who was made the holiest man and was to not carry a consciousness of offence, had to confess his sins and the sins of the Israelites[86]. Nehemiah confessed the sins of the Jews[87]. The people confessed their sins[88]; Daniel, the highly favored righteous man of God, prayed and confessed the sins of the people[89], which was a practice of his[90]; The psalmist taught in this manner regarding interaction with God when he said, "I will confess my transgressions," (Ps. 32:5), and, "I confess my iniquity" (Ps. 38:18). Solomon in His repentance said, "He who confesses will find mercy" (Prov. 28:13). In the time of Israel's return from captivity, they confessed and worshiped for one quarter of the day[91]. These examples

---

[84] (Lev. 5:5; Num. 5:7)
[85] (Jer. 3:13)
[86] (Lev. 16:21)
[87] (Neh. 1:6)
[88] (Lev. 26:40; Ezra 10:11; Neh. 9:2)
[89] (Dan. 9:4)
[90] (Dan. 9:20)
[91] (Neh. 9:3)

and many more in the Old Testament are given so that we may learn from them[92]. In the New Testament, the people of God are observed under the conviction of the Holy Spirit, confessing their sins, and were baptised by John[93]. Even in the prayer that He taught His disciples, He emphasized repentance when He said, "Forgive us of our sins as we forgive everyone who is indebted to us" (Luke 11:4). The Ephesians confessed their deeds[94]. Once again, we are called to confess our sins to each other[95]. We are also to confess our sins to Christ Jesus, and He will forgive us[96].

There are those who would make everything in the Old Testament irrelevant to us today. However, we know that the things that are written are given to us as an example and reflection to heavenly things[97]. We cannot write off the Old Testament or even the Law; they were all expressions of God's love and mercy to humanity. There has never been anything legalistic about God's love. Since the time that Adam rebelled against God, He has extended His love, calling us back to Himself. One of the radical statements of Jesus was found in what He said about all that God has done in the past. Jesus said,

---

[92] (Rom. 15:4)
[93] (Matt. 3:6; Mark 1:5)
[94] (Acts 19:18)
[95] (Jas. 5:16)
[96] (1 John 1:9)
[97] (Rom. 15:4, Heb 8:5, 10:1)

> "Do not suppose that I have come to abolish the Law or the prophets. I did not come to abolish, but to fulfill. I tell you for certain that until Heaven and Earth shall pass away, not one iota or even a letter of the Law shall pass away until it all comes to pass. Whoever then shall break one of the least of these commandments and shall teach men so shall be least in the Kingdom of Heaven, but whoever shall practice and teach them shall be called great in the Kingdom of Heaven" (Mt. 5:17-19).

Jesus also said,

> "As many as I love, I rebuke and correct. Be zealous then and repent. Behold, I stand at the door and knock, if anyone hears My voice and opens the door, I will come in to him and will dine with him and he with Me. He who overcomes I will give him to sit with Me in My throne, as I also overcame sat down with My Father in His throne" (Rev. 3:19-21).

What we can confidently conclude is that repentance is the means by which the blood is applied for our sins to be forgiven. The blood of the everlasting covenant never needs to be shed again. It remains viable, living, and effective forever. **If** we sin, we have an Intercessor, a great High Priest, the One Whose blood removes the sins that we confess and turn from. God is the same yesterday, today, and forever – He has not, and will not, ever change.

He hates sin as much as He always has. In His lovingkindness, He continues to offer a cleansing for sin through repentance and faith in the blood of Jesus. Just as Jesus told the church in Revelation to repent, even so He invites all in the church today to repent of their sins. Those who say that we do not need to repent if we sin have departed from the scripture. If indeed all need to repent of their sins to be forgiven, then those who don't retain their sins and are in danger of an eternity with the rest of those who refuse to humble themselves and who rebel against God. The Word of God that endures for every generation declares,

> **"I acknowledged my sin unto You, and my iniquity have I not hid. I said, 'I will confess my transgressions unto the LORD,' and You forgave the iniquity of my sin. Selah. For this shall everyone that is godly pray to You in a time when You may be found" (Ps. 32:5–6).**

The ongoing ministry of our great High Priest, Christ Jesus, is captured throughout the Epistle to the Hebrews. Christ Jesus is a "merciful and faithful High Priest in things pertaining to God, to make reconciliation for the sins of the people" (Heb. 2:17). This verse is referring to the covenant people under the Old Testament, and it represents what Christ Jesus would be for us in the New Testament. The intercessory ministry of Jesus for us now takes us right back to the Old Testament type in which the High Priest officiated in offering the blood of sacrifice for the people's sins any time they were committed. This verse of scripture in Hebrews 2:17 highlights two major New Testament doctrines: 1- The High Priest ministry of Jesus, and 2- how He deals with the sins of the redeemed. First of all we know that Jesus is forever a High Priest[98].

With regards to His priestly ministry for the sins of His people, we know that He entered once with His blood into the Holy of Holies to obtain eternal redemption[99]. There will never be the need again for another sacrifice. Christ Jesus is the Mediator and Intercessor for any sins that we should commit. He forever officiates the New Covenant with His own blood. He entered once with His blood, and we know that His blood remains in force to cleanse anyone who comes to Him for a cleansing from sins.

If a person who is born again sins, their sins will be cleansed by our great High Priest if they renounce the sins and turn away from them. The effectiveness of the blood only becomes viable when confession and transmission of the sins has been made to the sacrifice[100].

As the type, so is the antitype. We confess our sins, and that sin is transferred to Christ Jesus, Who bore it 2,000 years ago, and His blood is efficacious to cleanse us from

---

[98] (Ps. 110:4; Hebrews 4:14-15; 5:1–10; Heb. 3:1; 6:20; 7:1, 26–27; 8:1, 3; 9:11, 25; 10:21; 13:11)
[99] (Hebrews 9:12)
[100] (Lev. 4:3, 14, 23, 28, 33, 5:6, 8, 10, 15; 7:17; 8:14; 9:1-22)

all unrighteousness[101]. There is no need for Him to offer His blood again, as was necessary under the Law, because His blood is forever and eternally viable to cleanse. He entered once into the Holy Place as the High Priest did for Yom Kippur and obtained an eternal redemption for the cleansing of the Holy Place for past sins[102]. Yet, this was not the end of the priestly ministry. Any time that a person sinned, they would bring a sacrifice of their sins, and the priest would make intercession for their sins[103]. In Christ Jesus's priestly ministry, He purges our conscience from works of death (νεκρῶν ἔργων, 'nekron ergon') so that we may worship the living God[104]. Jesus did several things with His blood:

1 – He ratified the New Covenant [105].

2 – He purified the heavenly Holy of Holies – as was more perfectly described with the type on Yom Kippur –for the redemption of the transgression under the first covenant[106].

3 –He administers the everyday intercession ministry for the sins of the people[107].

4 – There is a demonstration of the application of the blood to our own lives first in Passover. Jesus is

---

[101] (1 Peter 2:24)
[102] (Heb 9:23)
[103] (Heb 9:24; 2:17)
[104] (Heb 9:14; Romans 12:1)
[105] (Heb. 9:16-21; Ex 24:7-8; 40; Lev 8, 1 Peter 1:2)
[106] (Hebrews 9:23-24, 15)
[107] (Heb. 2:17; 8:2; 9:11; 24; Lev 17:11; Mt 26:28; 1 John 1:9)

our Passover Lamb and as our Passover Lamb we apply His blood to our lives as those in Egypt placed the blood of their lambs on their houses so that death would not enter[108]. The blood was sprinkled upon the people when the first covenant was ratified[109]. Each time we participate with the Lord's supper, which was commemorated by the Lord on Passover, we testify to His blood being applied to our lives[110].

5 – The blood of the Lamb is revealed to be one of our primary battle weapons against Satan[111].

To come to a place where we say that sin has no penalty is deception. That there is a penalty for sin is underscored time and time again from the first lesson of Scripture to the last[112]. The need for the act of turning from sin, and the need for the blood of Jesus for cleansing, are beyond question. If we sin and pretend that there is no need to confess or acknowledge the sin, then we are trampling the blood of the covenant underfoot, totally disregarding why it was shed. If we sin presumptuously as though there is nothing really wrong with it, or that it's

---

[108] (Ex. 12:21-23; 1 Cor 5:7; Mt 26:27-28; 1 Cor 11:25)
[109] (Ex. 24:7-8; 30:25-30; 1 Peter 1:2; Heb 10:22; 12:24; Lev. 8:10, 15, 30)
[110] (1 Cor. 11:23-30)
[111] (Rev. 12:11)
[112] (Gen. 2:15, Rev. 22:12)

somehow overlooked by God, then it's trampling the blood of the covenant underfoot[113].

There is a presumptuous sin that disregards what God says and arrogantly justifies whatever iniquity one chooses. When a person disregards the direct command of God they have engaged in treachery against the Lord[114]. There is a total disregard for God's judgment against sin and no remorse for one's actions. Presumption says, "God does not see, neither does He regard it" (Ps. 94:7). The claim is that judgment or a penalty for sin is not justified. It is a sin in which a person has been clearly instructed that it is not to be done, yet is unwilling to turn from it. Some of its meaning is found with those who "hold the truth of God in unrighteousness" (Rom. 1:18); and also with those who would "turn the grace of God into lasciviousness" (Jude 1:4); or who would say, "Let us sin that grace may abound" (Rom 6:1; 3:8). They have moved past conviction, and even with pious stubbornness, they claim that they are right when they are wrong.

Hebrews chapter 10 is about the cleansing blood of Christ Jesus and His priestly ministry. It is a call to come before God boldly, confidently, with a true heart, in full assurance of the faith by the blood of Jesus. If we are unwilling to repent and take hold of the blood of Jesus for our cleansing, then there remains a fearful and fiery

---

[113] (Heb. 10:29)
[114] (Deut 1:43; 17:12-13; 2 Peter 2:10)

judgment that will come upon us from the Father of our Lord Jesus Christ. Simply put, there is no other means to be cleansed from sin other than acknowledging the sin, allowing the blood to be applied by Jesus to our lives, and turning from it with our whole heart. If we are unwilling to do this, then there remains no more sacrifice – there's no other means of forgiveness. There is no other way in which God transforms the actions of our lives. Hebrews 10:26-27 states:

> "For **if** we sin willfully/intentionally/deliberately (ἑκουσίως, hekousios') after that we have received the knowledge of the truth, there remains no more sacrifice for sins, but a certain fearful looking for of judgment and fiery indignation, which shall devour the adversaries" (KJV)
>
> "For **if** we go on sinning deliberately after receiving the knowledge of the truth, there no longer remains a sacrifice for sins, but a fearful expectation of judgment, and a fury of fire that will consume the adversaries" (ESV)
>
> "For we—wilfully sinning after the receiving the full knowledge of the truth—no more for sins doth there remain a sacrifice, but a certain fearful looking for of judgment, and fiery zeal, about to devour the opposers" (YLT)

"For if we willingly continue in sin after receiving the knowledge of the truth, there remains no more sacrifice for sin. But a fearful expectation of judgment and fierce fire that will consume the adversaries." (TOT)

Repentance is the recognition that sin is evil and a great violation of God's life. Unless a person recognizes that sin is wrong and really a great evil, there will be no repentance. Without this kind of repentance, there will be no transformation of a person's actions. As long as sin is justified, then a person remains in bondage to it. Some justify it by saying, "we are all sinners." Others justify sin by saying that Jesus died for our future sins because He knew we would continue on sinning. It doesn't matter what approach a person takes in justifying sin, the results are the same.

As long as a person is alive, God's mercy always reaches out. He is long-suffering, but remains uncompromising. God is merciful to all and in His goodness desires to teach us His ways. If we stumble, God has provided for us the most costly cleansing for our sin: the blood of His only begotten Son. Once again, to believe that the born-again believer does not need to repent or ask for forgiveness for sin is a tragic mistake. We must all recognize that would be a damnable error, if indeed sins must be confessed and turned from! The evidence that this is indeed the case is monumentous in Scripture. The Scripture so emphasizes this act of repentance that we would need a clear statement from God that it was no longer necessary. Instead, we have just the opposite – this is no place to make an error. Repentance – or, asking for forgiveness – for sins is established over and over again in both the Old and New Testament.

If you sin after that you are born again, you need to confess those sins and turn from them to be forgiven. Remember: 1 John 1:7 & 9 are for the believer; Revelation 3:19 is for the believer; 2 Corinthians 7:9-10 are for the believer; and James 5:16 is for the believer. Jesus addresses our need to forgive as we are forgiven, which is for the believer. James 1:12-15 and Romans 6:16, among many other scriptures, establish a serious consequence that the believer is in jeopardy of if they sin. If a person does not recognize the sin and renounce it, then how will it be addressed as an offense to God? How is a person ever supposed to express hatred for sin if there is no spoken declaration and recognition that God hates it? Where is there a verbal agreement with God about His will and a brokenness about sin if it's ignored? There is a miracle in repentance! There is a miracle when we confess it and the blood is applied – it's a miracle of the application of the blood of Jesus upon our lives that is transformative in action.

There is no scriptural reason to think that acknowledging sin and turning from it has anything at all to do with a works-based salvation. Grace does not make sin something less than the evil that it has always been to God. While it is true that Jesus's blood has washed all our sins away, we must also recognize that sin is not supposed to be in our lives. Turning away from sin is not works-based salvation – it's obedience to God; it's the fruits of righteousness and the evidence of a changed life[115]. If someone wants to say that the act of turning away from sin is not repentance, then they are simply playing a game of semantics. Repentance is not the abusive function of a guilty conscience – it's the gift of God's grace to be set free from the consequence of treason against God and His Kingdom. Acknowledgment of sin is not based on subjective thinking of the conscience, but is specifically found in the written Word of God and the conviction of the Holy Spirit. His law has been written on our hearts and minds to do them, so we most certainly would know when we are not doing them[116].

There is a belief that sin no longer affects our relationship with God. However, such an idea does not exist anywhere in Scripture. Instead, everywhere we look, sin has a terrible consequence. There is no question that demonic power and a demonic claim is associated with all

---

[115] (Php. 1:11, Eph. 4:5-10; Acts 26:20; Rev 2:5; Lk 3:8)
[116] (Heb 8:10; 10:16; 2 Cor. 3:3 etc.)

sin. God lists the sins that separate us from Himself many times, but especially in the New Testament. There is no subjectivity: Paul is very specific about what sin is, and he makes it very clear to everyone that those who practice such things have no inheritance in God. Are we really supposed to believe that there is a born-again Christian who has the Spirit of God and they are not grieved by sin? The Holy Spirit is certainly grieved by sin – He even groans over our weaknesses so that we may groan with Him[117]. Anyone who walks after their own ungodly lusts does not have the Spirit of God[118]. Anyone who does not hate and abhor evil does not have the Spirit of God in them[119].

We are given the gift of righteousness to walk in righteousness[120]. We have been made the righteousness of God to be righteous[121]. Everyone who does righteousness is righteous even as He is righteous. The one who sins is of the Devil[122]. There is no one who can practice sin and claim to be righteous. You cannot walk in darkness and claim to be born again. John makes this so repetitively clear in his first epistle that it's impossible to overlook it. Yet, as God's children, if we fall prey to sin, God has provided the remedy. God grants a cleansing from sin so

---

[117] (Eph. 4:30, Romans 8:25-26)
[118] (Jude 1:18)
[119] (Rom. 12:9; Isa 11:2-3; Ps 97:10)
[120] (Rom. 5:17-18; 8:4; 1 John 2:29; 1 Cor 1:31; Rom 4;17, etc.)
[121] (Romans 3:21; 2 Cor 5:21; 1 John 3:10; 1 Tim. 6:11; etc.)
[122] (1 John 3:7-8)

that everything about our relationship moves forward and develops into the fullness of the measure of Christ Jesus[123]. He gives us the full assurance of faith through the blood of Jesus to come to the throne of grace and enter the Holy of Holies. We do not have to run and hide as Adam did. We do not have to cover our transgression and act as though nothing is wrong in order to be right with God. It is unbelief to think that God will not instantaneously cleanse us from our sins when we ask Him. Faith in the blood allows us to be void of offense and free of all guilt and shame[124]. God gives us a perfect salvation and allows us to grow in grace as He perfects everything about our lives[125].

It is not somehow a godly action to ignore the reality that God hates sin and that it is an abomination to Him. God knows our works, and He therefore makes it very clear that we will give an account for the deeds done in our lives[126]. We all have a responsibility to God and must be ready to give an account to Him before the judgment seat of Christ[127]. God has made a perfect covenant that He finds no fault with. He changed our lives and has given us the life of Jesus Christ. He gave us the power of His own Holy Spirit to live out our lives before Him in

[123] (1 John 1:7, 9, Heb. 2:17: Rev. 1:5; Mt. 26:27 etc.)
[124] (Acts 24:16, Heb 10:2)
[125] (2 Peter 3:18; Jude 24; Col 1:22; 1 Peter 5:10; 2 Tim 3:17; Eph 4:11-12 etc.)
[126] (Rev. 2:2, 9, 13, 19, 23; Rom 2:16; Mt 12:36; Jn 12:48)
[127] (2 Cor. 5:10; Rom 14:10; 1 Cor 4:5; Ps 62:12 etc.)

righteousness and holiness[128]. The only way that anyone could believe that repentance is a works-based salvation is that they refuse to believe that we have been given the power and ability to walk in the Holy Spirit and live the life of Jesus – not by our own strength, but by His Spirit. We have been given the divine nature, and through His divine power God has given us all things that pertain to His life and godliness; to walk in the excellence of His character[129].

---

[128] (Luke 1:75; Eph. 4:24; Titus 2:12 etc.)
[129] (2 Peter 1:3-4, 9-10)

# Chapter 9

# *The Awfulness of Sin*

God is holy in all of His ways and righteous in all of His works. He has purer eyes than to behold evil and will have no fellowship with darkness or iniquity of any kind. Everything about Him is humble and lowly. There is only goodness and kindness in Him. The essence of Who He is is holiness, and the essence of His holiness is love. There is no variableness with God. He is forever the same, the unchanging God. His judgments are true, and everything about His ways are blameless. He created men to walk with Him and be like Him. Yet men have sinned and transgressed against the Almighty. They have made their ways crooked and turned aside to iniquity and everything that opposes God and His ways. They have done things that never entered into God's mind that they would do [130]. They have altogether perverted their ways. Yet God continues to reach out to mankind and invite them to

---

[130] (Jer. 7:32; 19:5; 32:35)

return unto Him. Look at all the evils and wickedness that one act of sin has resulted in. Everything about sin is as opposite to God as Satan himself is. There is nothing in the realms of sin and iniquity that can ever be justified.

God will not have sin in the universe that He created. It will be altogether done away with and will never exist again. He will have a new heaven and a new earth in which only righteousness dwells[131]. The heavens that now exist will pass away and the elements will melt with a fervent heat as the wrath of God brings an end to wickedness in His Universe[132]. Though men hate Him and blaspheme His holy name, still He reached out to all mankind to save them and heal them of their sin and iniquity. Anyone who has the fear of the Lord is going to recognize God's extreme and unwavering hatred of sin. It is wisdom to realize that sin results in death and therefore we would be wise to flee from it. God's judgment has been executed against sin in the past and will be in the future. People are falling into hell by the multiplied thousands every day.

Sin is a problem and was highlighted as the biggest issue of all in the first lesson of Scripture[133]. One act of sin opened the door for Satan to take control of man and all that God had placed under Adam's dominion. This great upheaval resulted in all of the death and destruction that

---

[131] (2 Peter 3:13; Isa 65:17)
[132] (2 Peter 11-12)
[133] (Gen. 2:15)

is witnessed even unto this day. Unless we properly understand the horrific darkness of sin and the Satanic realm, we will not begin to understand God's disposition toward it. If we do not recognize God's feeling and disposition toward sin, we will not understand and value the great gift of repentance. We will never grasp the magnitude of the forgiveness that we have received from a righteous and holy God if we cannot appreciate the great abomination that sin is to Him. Just as the serpent was lifted up on a pole in the wilderness, which was emblematic of the deadly poison of the bite of sin, even so Jesus was lifted up to show the just physical penalty for sin and endure the death that sin brings. When we view the horrific nature of how Christ Jesus was brutally treated and tortured, we are viewing the just penalty for sin. The prophet Isaiah said that His appearance was so marred that it was difficult to discern that He was a man[134].

> "The one thing which God hates is sin. It grieves and provokes Him, and He will destroy it. The one thing that makes man unhappy is sin. The one thing which Jesus had to give His blood for was sin. In all the communication between the sinner and God, this is the first thing which the sinner must bring to his God—sin." (Andrew Murray: Confession of Sin)

---

[134] (Isa. 52:14-15)

God expressed repeatedly His hatred and abhorrence for sin through His prophets[135]. He will have no association with it and has made it plain that His wrath and judgment is on sin. He will not allow it to exist in His eternal Kingdom. Jesus did not die to make sin right – He died to destroy sin and its claim on everyone who is willing to be recreated in Christ Jesus. Certainly, the righteousness of God was revealed from Heaven when Jesus came, died, and rose again from the dead, but the wrath of God was also revealed against all who hold the truth in unrighteousness[136].

Sin is so terrible that God created a place called Hell to contain it forever. Hell is certainly no minor subject of Scripture, with more than 50 references to it. Jesus told sinners and the religious alike that they would not escape the damnation of Hell if they refused to change. He made it painfully clear when He said, "if your eye causes you to sin pluck it out, if your hand causes you to sin cut it off, if your foot causes you to sin cut it off, for it would be better to go into life maimed than to be cast into the flames of hell" (Mt. 5:29-30; 18:9-9; Mark 9:45). It appears that it was a sermon that was commonly preached by Jesus. Even in the commission to go and preach to the world, not only are we to preach that good news of redemption, but we are

---

[135] (Ps. 97:10, Prov. 8:13; Amos 5:15; Micah 3:2; Lev 18:26, 29, 30; Deut 7:25-26; Ps 53:1; Prov. 15:9 etc 176 times)
[136] (Rom. 1:17-18)

also to declare the warning that those who reject the Gospel will be damned, because salvation is in no other name.

> "And He said to them, 'Go into all the world and preach the Gospel to every creature. He who believes and is baptized shall be saved, but he who does not believe shall be damned'" (Mk. 16:14–16).

There are those who think this is too harsh, but it's only because they refuse to recognize that God has made an opportunity for men to leave the realm of sin and come into the life that God created for them. It's not just about believing – it's about being born again and created anew in Christ Jesus. Those who refuse to change and come into God's Kingdom will suffer the same judgment that is on all sin.

The Apostle Peter, warning believers against sin, said that if God did not spare the angels who sinned, but cast them down to Hell, they should beware also[137]. The list that is given both by Peter and Jude is sizable. In the days of Noah, the whole of mankind was put to death. Those in the cities of Sodom and Gomorrah were put to death because of their wickedness. Even those who were brought into the covenant who rebelled were judged by God and put to death. If God judged them, why would anyone who continues in sin today think that they are going to escape

---

[137] (1 Pet. 2:4)

the judgment of God? Peter concludes his warning to sinning Christians by saying,

> "For if after they have escaped the pollution of the world through the knowledge of the Lord and Savior Jesus Christ, they are again entangled therein and overcome, the latter end is worse with them than the beginning. For it had been better for them not to have known the way of righteousness, than, after they have known it, to turn from the holy commandment delivered to them" (2 Pet. 2:20–21).

One of the main subjects of Scripture is sin. It has several related words: iniquity, wickedness, evil, transgression, darkness, abomination etc. In total, we find sin mentioned 749 times, iniquity 334 times, wickedness 449 times, transgression 149 times, darkness about 150 times, and abomination 176 times. In all, this is one of the more common concepts of Scripture, with a total of 2,007 references. It is made painfully clear in scripture that God's wrath abides on it and those who practice it will not inherit the Kingdom of God.

John 8 is devoted to one of the major sermons of the Gospels. Jesus tells the Jews that they will die in their sins, that they are from beneath, and that He is from above; that they are of the world, and He is not of the world; that they will die in their sins because they refused to believe that He was the Messiah Who would save them from their sins. He made it very clear that He was talking to those who were continuing on in sins[138]. He said that those who commit sins are the servants of sin. He told them that they were of their father the Devil[139]. Jesus made His position very clear when it came to dealing with the issue of sin.

In all of Jesus's teaching, He taught men about their need to repent of sin and to turn from it. Sin that separates from God and has His fiery judgment against is the most repeated subject in the Bible. The first lesson of Scripture is that sin brings forth death, and this lesson is repeated throughout the Word of God[140]. Death is a spiritual state in which Satan gains dominion over our lives through sin. It's impossible to escape the fact that θάνατος ('thanatos') is often used to express a state of spiritual death by Paul...

> "Don't you know, that to whom you yield yourselves servants to obey, his servants ye are to whom ye obey; whether of sin unto death, or of obedience unto righteousness" (Rom 6:16).

For Paul the act of yielding to sin was death "whether of sin unto death". Just as obedience resulted in righteousness. Paul's message is that to yield to sin is to give it dominion and to become a slave to it[141]. The result of sin is a spiritual uncleanness- "for as you have yielded your

---

[138] (John 8:34)
[139] (John 8:44)
[140] (Gen. 2:17, Rom. 6:23, Jam. 1:15)
[141] (Rom. 6:16-19, cr. 2 Pet. 2:19; *cr.* Rom. 8:13)

members servants to uncleanness and to iniquity unto iniquity" (Ro 6:19). Sin results in spiritual uncleanness, and to yield to iniquity results in iniquity in our lives. This has nothing whatsoever to do with a works based salvation and everything to do with walking in the liberty and freedom given to us by the Lord Jesus Christ[142]. Jesus was absolutely clear, "whoever practices sin is the servant of sin" (Jn 8:34). Peter said,

> "While they promise them liberty, they themselves are the servants of corruption: for of whom a man is overcome, of the same is he brought in bondage. For if after they have escaped the pollutions of the world through the knowledge of the Lord and Saviour Jesus Christ, they are again entangled therein, and overcome, the latter end is worse with them than the beginning (2 Pe 2:19–20).

The same message was repeated by all of the other writers of the New Testament (example: 1 Jn. 3:8; James 1:12-15; Jude 1:1-19).

Paul told us that the wages of sin is death[143]. He said that those who sin are worthy of death[144], and that the end of sin is death[145]. If you live after the flesh you shall die[146].

---

[142] (John 8:36)
[143] (Rom 6:23)
[144] (Rom 1:32)
[145] (Rom 6:21)
[146] (Rom 8:13)

Some discount this as something that is no longer true, but James, the half-brother of Jesus, made it even more specific to the believer. He said,

> "Then when lust <u>gives birth to sin</u> (τίκτει ἁμαρτίαν, 'tiktei hamartion'); and sin, when it is finished, <u>gives birth to death</u> (ἀποκύει θάνατον, 'apokuei thanaton') (James 1:15).

While sin is clearly revealed to result in a spiritual death, we know that God gives us a space and time to repent before a final judgment falls[147]. It's best to understand what Jesus, Paul, Peter, John and James said and turn from all sin and iniquity. Once again, God in His great love and mercy provided us with the ability to turn from it once and for all through the new birth. If we sin, God in His amazing love continues to provide us with the ability to turn from sin and have every effect of it removed from our lives and relationship with Him. God desires that "we "give no place to the Devil" (Eph. 4:27).

The proclamation of Jesus and the empowerment that is given to us is, "Go and sin no more" (John 5:14; 8:11). John said that we "keep ourselves and the wicked one cannot touch us" (1 John 5:18). Peter said that God gave us "all things that pertain to life and godliness." He gave us

---

[147] (Rev. 2:21; Rom 2:4; 2 Peter 3:9)

instruction on how to walk in this life and godliness so that we would not even stumble[148].

The story of Ananias and Sapphira is a tragic event. It is one of the most extreme examples of the consequence of sin. They thought they lied to a man about an offering, but found out that they were not lying to a man, but to the Holy Spirit. They did not realize that they were lying to the Holy Spirit – but regardless, the judgment was the same. When they had agreed together to hold back part of the offering that they had pledged to give and then lied about it, they discovered that their lie resulted in death. This is unique, because usually there is an opportunity to confess your sins and be forgiven. However, Ananias and Sapphira had an opportunity to confess before the Holy Spirit, but their confession was a lie, and they fell down dead. Peter addressed Ananias, asking him why he allowed Satan to fill his heart with a lie. Peter used similar language that we find in James, asking Ananias why he conceived in his heart to commit this egregious sinful act. This was a sinful act that resulted not just in spiritual death, but in physical death. Yes, Satan had filled his heart, but he was also responsible for opening his heart to it just as Eve was responsible for opening her heart to sin. Although there was demonic deception that took place, the final decision rests with the individual who acts on the temptation. Together, Ananias and Sapphira were being tempted by

---

[148] (2 Peter 1:4-10)

Satan, but ultimately their sin was an act of tempting the distinct person- the Holy Spirit. The result was, as James described, they conceived it in their heart and the act of sin resulted in death.

Paul says to every believer, "Let no man deceive you with vain words, for because of these things, the wrath of God comes upon the children of disobedience" (Eph. 5:6). Paul gives an abbreviated list of those who have no inheritance in the Kingdom of Christ and of God. He warns the believers not to be partakers with them. If there was no jeopardy of the believer receiving the same judgment, then the warning makes no sense at all. Paul clearly tells us not to partake with them in their sins[149]. The emphasis is that they, as well as we, were once in darkness, and should we partake, we would lapse back into the darkness that we once were in. There is just no room for argument – Paul said the unrighteous will not inherit the Kingdom of God[150].

The unrighteous are defined by their sin and iniquity even as the righteous are defined by their actions. Acts of unrighteousness, which are called the fruits of unrighteousness, are fruits of the spirit of disobedience[151]: fornication, and all uncleanness, or covetousness, let it not be once named among you, as is becoming for saints; filthiness, foolish talking, jesting, whoremongering,

---

[149] (Eph. 5:7)
[150] (1 Cor. 6:9)
[151] (Eph. 5:6)

uncleanness; the covetousness, idolaters, adulterers, effeminate, abusers of themselves with mankind, thieves, drunkards, revilers, extortioners; lasciviousness, witchcraft, hatred, variance, emulations, wrath, strife, seditions, heresies, envyings, murders, false witness, blasphemies, jealousy, slander, lying, hypocrisy… which pretty much sums up what goes on in the world around us. Acts of Righteousness, which are called the fruits of righteousness, are fruits of the Spirit[152]: love, joy, peace, longsuffering, gentleness, goodness, faith, meekness, temperance, holiness, purity, excellence of character; knowledge, patience, godliness, brotherly kindness, humility, lowliness, forgiveness, mercy, truth, and being a peacemaker.

We are called to walk in the light as Christ Jesus is in the light. We are to walk as children of the light and to prove what is acceptable to God. We are to have no fellowship with the unfruitful works of darkness, but are to rebuke them. We were once darkness, but now we are light. If anyone says that they have fellowship with God and walk in darkness, they are a liar. Walking in the light is analogous to walking in righteousness, even as walking in darkness is analogous to walking in unrighteousness. In fact, Paul tells us not to associate with a person who calls himself a brother and is a "fornicator, or greedy, or an idolater, or a slanderer, or a drunkard, or a thief – do not

---

[152] (Eph. 5:9)

even eat with them" (1 Cor. 5:11). Doing so would indicate fellowship with the unfruitful works of darkness.

The wages of sin is death. Disobedience to God still results in death, whether it is a person who is a Christian or not. The difference is that God in His great mercy and love has granted unlimited forgiveness to those who ask for it. Forgiveness is not granted unless we acknowledge the sin and repent. God has never looked the other way when sin was committed. He has never justified the wicked, and He never will. He is God and He does not change. Everywhere in Scripture, there was a consequence for sin. When sin was committed, God commanded that an innocent victim had to die to make restitution for that sin. Today, when men sin, there remains no more sacrifice for sin. The blood of Jesus forever remains as the means by which men's sins are forgiven. If we sin and we confess that sin, Christ Jesus is faithful and just to cleanse us from all unrighteousness with His purifying blood.

# Chapter 10

# *Unlimited Forgiveness*

There is no limit to God's mercy and loving-kindness – His mercy is new every morning. It is so vast that it is described as being in the heavens. God's mercy towards us will never fail. The very way of God's holiness is mercy and loving-kindness. If we will trust in the Lord, His mercy will surround us[153]. We can rejoice knowing that goodness and mercy will follow us all the days of our lives and that we will dwell in His house forever. Even though sin and iniquity are everything that God hates and are extreme violations of His life and treason against His Kingdom, yet He stands ready to forgive and deliver all who come to Him in repentance. Everything in the world is opposite to God's holiness, but He is willing to forgive, cleanse, and teach us the right way – the good way. All we have to do is repent and turn from sin.

---

[153] (Ps. 32:10)

The unfathomable love of God was fully demonstrated in Christ Jesus. God, the eternal Word, laid aside His eternal glory and majesty. He made Himself nothing to redeem us. He took on the form of a servant to bring all who would believe back into His Kingdom. For God so loved the world that He sent His Son to be the offering of sin for us. Jesus went to the cross with joy for our sake so that we might be freed from the powers of sin and death that shackled us. He bore all of our sorrows and carried all of our griefs. He was manifested to destroy the works of darkness that set themselves against us to plague us with every form of death. The King of Glory willingly laid His life down to become the servant of all to reveal the love of the Father and show all – whosoever will – the way back into the family of God. The One Who never knew any kind of sin became the sin-offering for every person so that we might be made the righteousness of God in Him.

When we were the enemies of God by wicked works, God loved us beyond words and Christ Jesus died for us. The Lord has supplied all of His fullness to us and packaged it together in knowing and believing the love that God has for us[154]. God Almighty revealed to Moses the commitments of His love for us. He revealed that He is merciful, gracious, longsuffering, full of loving-kindness and truth. The mercy of God knows no end to those who will love Him and desire to be part of the life that He

---

[154] (Eph. 3:19)

created. There is nothing that can separate us from the love of God as long as we are willing to receive His help and be part of His family.

Even if we rebel against God and refuse to listen, He still pursues us. He found us worthless and without hope, and He reached out to love us, ransom us, and invite us into His family. The prophet Ezekiel describes who we are and what God did for us when he found us as an aborted child, unlovely and unwanted: "And when I passed by you and saw you polluted in your own blood, I said unto you when you were in your blood, 'Live!' Yes, I said unto you when you were in your blood, 'Live!'…Then I washed you with water – yes, I thoroughly washed away your blood from you, and I anointed you with oil. I also clothed you with embroidered work and placed upon you badgers' skin, and I clothed you with fine linen, and I covered you with silk. I also decorated you with ornaments, and I put bracelets upon your hands, and a chain on your neck. And I put a jewel on your forehead, and earrings in your ears, and a beautiful crown upon your head. In this way you were decorated with gold and silver, and your clothing was of fine linen, silk, and embroidered work. You ate fine flour, honey, and oil…[155]

God demonstrated His abiding love and mercy to His people by example through the prophet Hosea. Just as His people had played the harlot and ran after other gods and

---
[155] (Eze. 16:6, 9–13)

all kinds of wickedness, Hosea would marry a woman who would do the same. God told Hosea to go and love a harlot named Gomer. She bore to the prophet three children: two sons and a daughter. Having grown tired of the prophet, she chased after other men to commit adultery with them. Similarly, God showed the amazing love and mercy He had toward His people and pursued Israel to purchase her and bring her back. He tried to restrain her from pursuing her lovers, but nothing that He did could stop her. God told Hosea to go and find Gomer and purchase her so that she would not play the harlot and would be content to stay with him for many days[156]. It did not matter how wicked His people behaved, He loved them and did everything that He could to bring them to Himself – but they would not heed Him. Finally, it came to a point where he had to judge that wicked generation, because they had grown so wicked and obstinate against God that there remained no more hope to persuade them. So He gave them over to their own sin and wickedness that consumed them. So long as there was hope, His mercy did not fail. When there was no hope, He found a small remnant that He could preserve, just as He found Noah among the wicked.

---

[156] (Hosea 1-3)

# Chapter 11

# *This Covenant Has No Fault*

How can anyone find fault with a covenant that God can find no fault with? God did not leave mankind in their sinful state, bound by the powers of darkness, but He delivered them. He did not leave mankind with an evil and sinful heart, but He gave all who would receive a new heart. He did not leave man in the spiritual death that resulted in the spirit of man being under the power of the spirit of darkness, but He created a new spirit. God gave us His own Holy Spirit through the person the Holy Spirit to help us and teach us to walk in His way of life. All of the power of God has been mobilized to give us the ability to live our lives in His ways. He has given to us all things that pertain to His life and godliness so that we can be all that He has purposed for our life in Him[157]. He is able and

---

[157] (2 Peter 1:3)

committed to save us to the uttermost who come to Him by His Son[158].

God, in His love, has established unlimited mercy for every sin that man has committed or might commit. All that anyone must do is put their trust in Christ Jesus and be willing to learn the ways of the life that God created. God has made provision to forgive everyone who is willing to recognize their sin and turn from it. He has supplied an unlimited number of times for a person to be forgiven. God does not run out of mercy for those who desire it as long as they are willing to turn from their sin and iniquity and to learn righteousness. If a person sins and then repents, God will turn and forgive them seven times seventy[159]. His love is so extended to us that He forever lives to intercede for us. His love and commitment for us is so great that He laid aside all of His power and eternal glory to become a baby in a manger. He left all of His honor and might to grow as a man and find only humiliation and rejection. He loved us so much that He let men brutally beat Him then hang Him on a tree to bear away our sins. He went down into Hell, and there, having won the keys of death, arose from the dead to raise us up together with Him. He ascended up on high to receive a name greater than any other name and to be placed once again upon the throne of Heaven. There He secured our

---

[158] (Heb 7:25)
[159] (Mt 18:21-22)

place in Himself, taking all that He Himself had won – all that He had by Himself purchased – to give us His own name. His Father became our Father – His God became our God. He made us co-inheritors to all that He inherited. He has invited us to the throne that He was given so that we may sit down on His throne even as He sat down on His Father's throne. He gave us His name, His power, and His authority. He won gifts for us, and by His blood He purchased for us the greatest gift: the gift of the Holy Spirit. After supplying us with a brand new life and the divine power to live it – after having given us all the luxuries of Heaven – if we for a second should cast them aside, He is there to plead with us to return to Him and continue in the way of life. If we betray Him, He still loves us. If we commit treason against our Father and His Kingdom, He stands by our side to make intercession as our Advocate. Our Heavenly Father, Who spared not His own Son, but offered Him up for us all, shall also freely give us all things by Him[160].

There are those who think that God's love and mercy are different now than it was in the times before Jesus. That somehow God's judgment against sin is different. They fail to realize that God's evaluation of Himself is that He does not change[161]. However, God's anger and wrath against sin is the same as it was from the beginning. Paul

---
[160] (Rom. 8:32)
[161] (Malachi 3:6; James 1:17; 2 Peter 3:8)

refers many times to the judgment and wrath of God that is revealed against sin and warns men of sins consequences[162]. There is a philosophical concept of God among Christians that sin and hell no longer exist. It is believed that know one should feel bad about sinning against God. They believe that grief and the pain of godly sorrow is a token of unbelief. They believe that remorse for sin and godly sorrow is not a New Testament doctrine. They feel there should be no godly sorry or conviction for sin that results in a person coming under conviction. To experience shame even for a second is more than they can bear or believe is just. To have to consider themselves as a failure because of allowing iniquity in their lives is more than they should have to endure. They think it's wrong to announce the judgments of God against sin and make it a violation against the God of love and grace. They consider Hell as something that does not represent the judgments of God, and they think it's improper to speak of it. Unlike the One they call their Master, they refuse to call out sin and warn men of an eternity in Hell, where its flames never stop burning and the torment for sin never ceases.

So many people find it impossible to reconcile the God Who loves so deeply with His judgment against sin, only because they know nothing of how evil – how unimaginable and horrific – sin is to God. The smallest act

---

[162] (Rom 1:18, 32; 2:3,5,8,12; Eph 5:6; Heb 10:27; 13:4; 1 Pet. 4:17; 2 Pet 2:9; 3:7; Jude 15)

of sin before God is more wicked than anyone can imagine, yet God remains merciful. To begin to understand God's holiness is to begin to understand the greatness of sin's violation against the very existence of life itself. Its crime goes beyond any punishment that can be reckoned. The only way to stop this death and enemy of life is to contain it within a flame – in which the sin itself cannot exist – forever. Even the bodies of these wicked ones must be raised from the Earth, that they too may be erased from all existence forever. That is the ultimate expression of just how evil sin is. This is the judgment of the most loving person in all the universe. It is the description of just how horrific sin is. Instead of making God unjust with regard to His judgment concerning sinners in Hell for eternity, we should instead understand through His righteous judgment just how terrible sin is.

# Chapter 12

## *Forgiven*

Although men have violated the ways of God and have opposed Him throughout their generations, He is always ready to forgive. In the justice of God, there was only one way to forgive those who committed crimes worthy of death: and that was to provide a substitute offering. God provided a means for someone to die in their stead, an innocent one that would bear their sins away. In this, the full payment for their sins would be rendered, and they would be able to go free in the justice system of God. It's difficult for many to understand that sin of any kind incurs the death penalty, because they have never really understood how evil sin is. If sin was allowed to run its full course, all of life would be destroyed. Although mens' behavior is only one small reflection of this truth, still we see men always on the verge of self-annihilation through war, hatred, greed, pride, and every form of self gratification. It's only the hand of God that restrains men from total self-destruction.

One of the great revelations of who God is can be found in the declaration: "God is love." God keeps mercy for thousands, forgiving iniquity, transgressions, and sins. He keeps mercy for those who love Him for a thousand generations. One of the beautiful attributes of love is forgiveness. When the Lord forgives, He forgives completely. His love is perfect, and His forgiveness is also perfect. He removes our sins as far as the East is from the West to remember them no more. He pours His love into our hearts so that we can know that we are forgiven. He provides faith and confidence so that we can have boldness and a full assurance about what we mean to Him and how completely forgiven we are. He comforts us and gives us a strong defence against every accusation and accusing spirit that would rise to condemn us.

Every sin-offering that was offered to bear the sins of those who sought forgiveness from God all pointed to and represented that one day God Himself would be the One to carry our sins – that in His earnestness to rid us of our sins and forgive our sins, He would carry them away for every person. He has now supplied forgiveness of sins through His blood. Can there be a more profound expression of love than the eternal Word, Who became the only begotten Son, supplying His own blood to provide forgiveness? God certainly redeemed us with the deepest expression of love possible. It is His blood that is there to supply us with the forgiveness that we may need. Just as in the time under the Law, there is a blood-penalty to pay for any sin committed. The blood that is supplied to us today is the precious blood of Jesus. Christ Jesus did not die as our substitute as the sacrifices of old but we were crucified together with Him. We died with Him, so that we might be raised to life with Him now by the spiritual and inward resurrection. We are now alive together with Him and are seated together with Him. As Paul said,

> "I am crucified with Christ: nevertheless I live; yet not I, but Christ lives in me: and the life which I now live in the flesh I live by the faith of the Son of God, who loved me, and gave himself for me" (Ga 2:20).

There are several Greek words that help us to understand the forgiveness supplied to us through the blood of Jesus, ἀφίημι ('aphiemi'), ἄφεσις ('aphesis'), χαρίζομαι ('charizomai'), and πάρεσις ('paresis'). These words reveal to us that our sins have been erased, wiped away, sent away, passed over, and canceled[163]. Even before the cross, Jesus revealed that He was the One Who had the power on Earth to forgive sins[164]. However, it was at the cross that He took on our sins in His own body – even the sins of the whole world – and put them to death[165]. The Lamb was slain for the sins of the world so that His blood

---

[163] (Col. 2:13; Mt 26:27; Eph 1:7; 4:32; Rom 3:25)
[164] (Luke 7:47; Mark 2:5)
[165] (1 Peter 2:24; 1 John 2:2)

would be made available to be applied to anyone who sought forgiveness for sins. The final sacrifice for cleansing was made, and the offering for sin would be forever available to be offered by the High Priest, Christ Jesus. Anyone who calls on the name of Jesus will find that He is a faithful High priest Who will make intercession for anyone who would come to God by Him[166].

> "Wherefore in all things it behooved Him to be made like unto His brethren, that He might be a merciful and faithful High Priest in things pertaining to God, to make reconciliation for the sins of the people" (Heb. 2:17).

When Adam and Eve sinned, the witness that God extended mercy to them was that they did not physically die for their sins at that moment. There was a sentence of death placed in their bodies but at that time they died spiritually. Physical death was postponed for Adam for 930 years. When they sinned God Himself made the first sacrifice to provide a covering for their nakedness and shame. Still, He could not allow them to remain in the glorious realm of His abundant life. He had to send them out, but with a promise of redemption. We know that God did not prohibit Adam or Eve from interacting with Him, because Abel, their son, displayed a fellowship with

---

[166] (Heb. 2:17; 7:25; Rom. 8:34)

God[167]. The same privilege was highlighted by Adam's grandson, Enos[168].

Forgiveness with God has always been made available to men[169]. God's willingness to forgive is highlighted by the many things that may be said about His loving nature toward all mankind. God is "ready to pardon, gracious and merciful, slow to anger, and of great kindness…"[170]

When you ask your Heavenly Father for forgiveness, He wants you to be confident that you are completely forgiven. That confidence should rest in the shed blood of Jesus Christ. He has given us the assurance of His love and faithfulness to forgive our sins in His only begotten Son, Jesus, Who gave His life for us and Whose blood was shed for our sins. He supplies the comfort of the Holy Spirit to give us confidence that we are forgiven and that we are His. When we were born again, He washed us and cleansed us with the greatest miracle possible – the washing of the water of regeneration. It's not possible to become more clean than to be created all over again. The former life with all of its sin was put to death by the miracle of redemption. The new life in Christ Jesus is a resurrected life, which testifies to a whole new beginning. As we were perfectly cleansed from our sins when we were

---

[167] (Gen 4:4)
[168] (Gen. 4:26)
[169] (Ps. 130:4)
[170] (Ne. 9:17 cr Numbers 14:18, Deuteronomy 4:31, Psalm 86:15, 103:8, 145:8-9, Joel 2:13, Jonah 4:2, Galatians 5:22-23, 2 Peter 3:9.)

born again, if we should fail in our walk with Him and sin, He washes it all away by faith in His blood so that fellowship is never lost. He continually supplies us with boldness through the blood of Jesus. We can always find ourselves with the ability to draw near to Him with a true heart in full assurance of the faith having the blood sprinkled upon our hearts[171].

Our forgiveness is all based on the love and faithfulness of God. God is unchanging – as He has been, He will forever continue to be. We should stand in awe of God's holiness and purity, and the essence of His holiness is His love. Forgiveness is one of the foremost expressions of God's love, and His love and forgiveness are eternal. God's commands to us – to demonstrate the attributes of His love by showing mercy and being forgiving – are essential for our continued relationship with Him. He is going to forgive us as long as we are also willing to forgive others. He has forgiven us a debt that really goes beyond calculation. However, in the parable of the unmerciful servant, he likens it to being forgiven for an impossible amount to ever repay. It would take about 60,000,000 days (over 164,000 years) of work for the unmerciful servant to pay off his debt to the king[172]. The judgment that came down upon him was severe. All that he had, including his wife and children, were to be sold to pay off the debt.

---

[171] (Heb 10:19-22)
[172] (Matthew 18:24)

When the servant sought for mercy from the king, the king forgave him all of his debt. This is a picture of our Heavenly Father.

There is reason for us to have an even greater assurance of forgiveness and acceptance with God more than any other time in history, for the blood of the only begotten Son was poured out to offer a guarantee that our sins are removed. We can be confident that as He has forgiven us in the past, He will also forgive us whenever we ask. God has filled us with His love. It's a love that is immeasurable and eternal. Today we live in His Kingdom under the ministry of righteousness in a relationship of oneness with Him.

The awesome restoration to the family of God that we have received has brought us into perfect union with God. He gave us a new heart and a new spirit and put the Holy Spirit in us. The Father, Christ Jesus, and the Holy Spirit now dwell in our lives. He has given us His righteousness and holiness. We are made sons of God and given sonship authority in Jesus.. He has made our bodies His temple and lives and walks in us. We are made one Spirit with the Holy Spirit. The Holy Spirit is our Teacher, Leader, and Guide. We live in Him, walk with Him, and are led by Him. Christ Jesus has baptized us in the Holy Spirit and fire and has given us His divine power to represent Him on the Earth. He has placed His life in us in such an amazing way that His presence and power flow out of us like rivers of life. Our heavenly Father has taken us beyond what Adam had. Adam was allowed the blessing of walking with God – now, God walks in us, as God has said, "I will dwell in them, and walk in them – and I will be their God, and they shall be My people" (2 Cor. 6:16).

Although we are not walking with God in the beauty of the garden that was made for Adam and Eve, we are walking with God in the beauty of His Spirit. He has clothed us with His righteousness and holiness and baptized us in the fire of His presence. He is our shelter and our hiding place and protection from all the darkness of this world. He has come not only to walk with us but also to walk in us and be our Perfector. He now dwells in our lives and is manifested through us as we yield our lives to Him. He has united our lives with His and fills up every part of our life. He raised us up above all of the powers of darkness and has set us at His own right hand in a heavenly realm. He has made us His heirs and co-inheritors with the last Adam, His only begotten Son, Jesus. He has filled us with His joy and peace and given us access into the holiest place where all His fullness dwells. Each one of us may now proclaim this song of victory. We are living in Heaven today – a far greater paradise than Adam knew, for this paradise is Christ Jesus. This walk with the living God is not just side-by-side, for He now dwells in me. He dwells in me and I dwell in Him, the glorious holy Trinity. Forever He dwells in me and I dwell in Him. The One Who is the express image of the Father has called me to the same – to every day be conformed to the image of His glory through His holy name. He, in Whom the fullness of the Godhead dwells, now dwells in me. So every day is Heavenly as I'm walking with His Majesty: the King of Kings, the Lord of Lords, Whose glory reigns forever.

# *Appendix*

**Some of the many theologians on the confession by Christians of sins to be cleansed.** The following citations are to emphasize that confession of sins is broadly accepted as a biblical doctrine across denominations. The majority believe that it is essential for forgiveness.

# Annabaptist

"confessing sin probably is inherited from Jewish religious culture, especially the process associated with the Day of Atonement (Lev. 16:21; cf. 5:5; Josh 7:19; Ps 32:5; Prov 28:13; Dan 9:20). In this OT context, the confession is made to God, the covenant partner offended by sin.
…What is clearer is the fact that the entire community is to engage in the confessing process."

**J. E. McDermond**, 1, 2, 3 John, Believers Church Bible Commentary (Harrisonburg, VA; Waterloo, ON: Herald Press, 2011), 67.

# Anglican

"confess our sins.... The author projects a situation in which people acknowledge their sins in an ongoing way. He portrays authentic Christian living as involving honest and ongoing acknowledgement of one's sins."
    **Colin G. Kruse**, The Letters of John, The Pillar New Testament Commentary (Grand Rapids, MI; Leicester, England: W.B. Eerdmans Pub.; Apollos, 2000), 68.

"The proper Christian attitude to sin is not to deny it but to admit it, and then to receive the forgiveness which God has made possible and promises to us"
    **John R. W. Stott**, The Letters of John: An Introduction and Commentary, vol. 19, Tyndale New Testament Commentaries (Downers Grove, IL: InterVarsity Press, 1988), 82.

"'I am a sinner;' but if confession is to have value it must state the definite acts of sin."
    **H. D. M. Spence-Jones**, ed., 1 John, The Pulpit Commentary (London; New York: Funk & Wagnalls Company, 1909), 5.

"The "confession" which characterizes a true penitent, of course is not to be understood of a mere acknowledgment, but an acknowledgment accompanied with suitable contrition, and with a humble faith in the Lord Jesus."

**Charles Simeon,** Horae Homileticae: James to Jude, vol. 20 (London: Holdsworth and Ball, 1833), 369.

"The plural is significant: we confess specific sins, not simply that we sin. And because God is faithful and just (cf. Dt. 32:4; Mi. 7:18–20; Rom. 3:25) he forgives."

**Leon L. Morris**, "1 John," in New Bible Commentary: 21st Century Edition, ed. D. A. Carson et al., 4th ed. (Leicester, England; Downers Grove, IL: Inter-Varsity Press, 1994), 1401.

"And the divine blessing connected with the confession of sins is twofold. It includes (1) the remission of sins, the remission of the consequences which they entail, and (2) the cleansing of the sinner from the moral imperfection which separates him from God: 1 Cor. 6:9; Luke 13:27"

**Brooke Foss Westcott,** ed., The Epistles of St. John: The Greek Text with Notes and Essays, 4th ed., Classic Commentaries on the Greek New Testament (London; New York: Macmillan, 1902), 23.

"So what can we do when we fall into sin? John says that we can confess our sins to God and receive his forgiveness and cleansing."

**Andrew Knowles**, The Bible Guide, 1st Augsburg books ed. (Minneapolis, MN: Augsburg, 2001), 687.

"but by confessing our sins, we cast ourselves on, we approach and put to the proof for ourselves, and shall find operative in our case, in the ἀφῇ and καθαρίσῃ, &c., those His attributes of faithfulness and justice."

**Henry Alford**, Alford's Greek Testament: An Exegetical and Critical Commentary, vol. 4 (Grand Rapids, MI: Guardian Press, 1976), 429.

# Baptist

"This lifestyle includes walking in the light (1:7), confessing sin (1:9), growing in holiness (2:1), keeping God's commandments (2:3–6), loving one another (2:7–11), and hating the things of the world and the flesh, or sinful nature (2:15–17)."

    **Ted Cabal et al.**, The Apologetics Study Bible: Real Questions, Straight Answers, Stronger Faith (Nashville, TN: Holman Bible Publishers, 2007), 1865.

"All believers must acknowledge their sin to God, the meaning of "confess," in order to experience Jesus' cleansing work"

    **Gary W. Derickson**, First, Second, and Third John, Evangelical Exegetical Commentary (Bellingham, WA: Lexham Press, 2012), 107.

"...so as we confess our sins not only are we forgiven, right, not only are we forgiven of our sin, ἀφῇ, but we also experience cleansing, purifying from unrighteousness, a transformative effect of God's forgiveness and the presence of His spirit."

    **Robert L. Plummer**, Daily Dose of Greek: Transcripts (Bellingham, WA: Faithlife, 2021), 1 Jn 1:9.

"John makes clear in 1:9 that it is those who confess their sins by believing in Jesus who have fellowship with the Father and fulfill the condition for fellowship"

    **Daniel L. Akin**, 1, 2, 3 John, vol. 38, The New American Commentary (Nashville: Broadman & Holman Publishers, 2001), 74.

"'if we keep on confessing.' Confession of sin to God and to one another (James 5:16) is urged throughout the N. T. from John the Baptist (Mark 1:5) on"

    **A.T. Robertson**, Word Pictures in the New Testament (Nashville, TN: Broadman Press, 1933), 1 Jn 1:9.

"He had been speaking of that in the eighth verse, but here he uses the plural to include both sin in its essence and in its actual development in our life. We are to confess both the inward sin and the outward fruit of it"

    **Charles Spurgeon**, Spurgeon Commentary: 1 John, ed. Elliot Ritzema, Spurgeon Commentary Series (Bellingham, WA: Lexham Press, 2014), 1 Jn 1:9

# Collection of Diverse Groups

"It is the nature of such repentance to make a change, and the greatest change as can be made here in the soul. Thus you see what repentance implies in its own nature; it denotes an abhorrence of all evil, and a forsaking of it. I shall now proceed…by the mercies of God in Christ Jesus, that you would no longer continue therein, but that you would forsake your evil ways, and turn unto the Lord, for he waiteth to be gracious unto you, he is ready, he is willing to pardon you of all your sins; but do not expect Christ to pardon you of sin, when you run into it, and will not abstain from complying with the temptations; but if you will be persuaded to abstain from evil and choose the good, to return unto the Lord, and repent of your wickedness, he hath promised he will abundantly pardon you, he will heal your back-slidings, and will love you freely."

**George Whitefield**: A Penitent Heart

"Forgiveness of the confessed sins is assured because God is 'faithful and just.'"
**Pedrito U. Maynard-Reid**, "Forgiveness," in Dictionary of the Later New Testament and Its Developments, ed. Ralph P. Martin and Peter H. Davids (Downers Grove, IL: InterVarsity Press, 1997), 380.

"In God's sight a man only becomes forgivable, that is, he only exhibits a moral attitude which can be forgiven, when he adopts God's point of view regarding sin [in repentance]."
**James Leo Garrett Jr.**, Systematic Theology: Biblical, Historical, and Evangelical, Second Edition, vol. 2 (Eugene, OR: Wipf & Stock, 2014), 324.

"Confession is inseparably linked with repentance; it is the outward expression to others of the inner admission to oneself that one was wrong in thought, word, attitude, or deed. It
**Jay Edward Adams**, From Forgiven to Forgiving (Wheaton, IL: Victor Books, 1989), 98."

"THE HERESY: DENIAL OF SIN
THE ANTIDOTE: CONFESSION OF SIN
If we confess (homologeo) our (hamartia) - IF introduces a third class conditional sentence which speaks of potential action. Confess (homologeo) in the present tense calls for continual confession and as such is a mark of a

genuine believer. John is not speaking of going into a booth and confessing to a man (such confession is not Biblical) who is also a sinner, but going to the throne of grace (Heb 4:16) and confessing to God. Failure to regularly confess one's sins should cause one to examine the authenticity of their salvation (2 Co 13:5+)!"

**Precept Austin**, https://www.preceptaustin.org/1john_19_commentary

"When the Holy Spirit begins to unearth the works of the flesh in you, don't temporize, don't whitewash them; don't call suspicion, "discernment of the spirit", or ill-temper, "righteous indignation"; bring it to the light, come face to face with it, confess it and get it cleansed away."

**Oswald Chambers**, Conformed to His Image

"Continued sinfulness and an unrepentant attitude bring great sorrow, but confession of sins and trusting in God for forgiveness bring great joy (32:10, 11). Certainly David's admonition concerning the importance of confessing sins is in line with the New Testament message that God will be faithful and just and forgive our sins if we will confess them to Him (1 John 1:9)."

**Samuel J. Schultz and Gary V. Smith**, Exploring the Old Testament (Wheaton, IL: Crossway Books, 2001), 124.

"...fellowship with the Father is interrupted, the way to correct this is to repent and seek forgiveness from their wives and be reconciled to them."
> **Jay Edward Adams**, From Forgiven to Forgiving (Wheaton, IL: Victor Books, 1989), 39.

"Perhaps it is best to distinguish between the judicial basis for the forgiveness of sins—the once-for-all work of Christ—and the continuing appropriation of the benefits of that sacrifice—through repeated repentance and confession of sins. Secured"
> **Douglas J. Moo**, "Confess, Confession," in Evangelical Dictionary of Biblical Theology, electronic ed., Baker Reference Library (Grand Rapids: Baker Book House, 1996), 112.

"In view of verse 8, Christians ought to be ready at all times to acknowledge any failure which God's light may expose to them. Thus John wrote, If we confess our sins, He is faithful and just and will forgive us our sins and purify us from all unrighteousness."
> **Zane C. Hodges**, "1 John," in The Bible Knowledge Commentary: An Exposition of the Scriptures, ed. J. F. Walvoord and R. B. Zuck, vol. 2 (Wheaton, IL: Victor Books, 1985), 885.

"When fellowship with the Father has been lost because of known sin, confession to Him results in the free granting of forgiveness and the restoration of fellowship, 1 John 1:9."

**William Evans and S. Maxwell Coder**, The Great Doctrines of the Bible, Enl. ed. (Chicago: Moody Press, 1974), 283.

"The proper Christian attitude to sin is not to deny it but to admit it, and then to receive the forgiveness which God has made possible and promises to us. If we confess our sins, acknowledging"

**John R. W. Stott**, The Letters of John: An Introduction and Commentary, vol. 19, Tyndale New Testament Commentaries (Downers Grove, IL: InterVarsity Press, 1988), 82.

"Unconfessed sin blocks the pathway of prayer to God and at the same time is a formidable obstacle in interpersonal relations. That means, confess your sins not only to God but also to the persons who have been injured by your sins. Ask them for forgiveness!"

**Simon J. Kistemaker and William Hendriksen**, Exposition of James and the Epistles of John, vol. 14, New Testament Commentary (Grand Rapids: Baker Book House, 1953–2001), 178.

"You must be willing to admit and confess the sin. Confession, repentance, and forgiveness are crucial elements in the healing process."
> **Tim Clinton and Ron Hawkins**, The Quick-Reference Guide to Biblical Counseling: Personal and Emotional Issues (Grand Rapids, MI: Baker Books, 2009), 211.

"Without the perception of sin no confession of sin, without confession of sin no forgiveness of sin, without forgiveness of sin no cancelling of sin"
> **John Peter Lange et al.**, A Commentary on the Holy Scriptures: 1, 2, 3 John (Bellingham, WA: Logos Bible Software, 2008), 41.

"John makes clear in 1:9 that it is those who confess their sins by believing in Jesus who have fellowship with the Father and fulfill the condition for fellowship."
> **Daniel L. Akin,** 1, 2, 3 John, vol. 38, The New American Commentary (Nashville: Broadman & Holman Publishers, 2001), 74.

"Gospel narratives take full account of the confession of sin, and that, as in the OT, confession is recognized both as the necessary accompaniment of repentance and as the indispensable condition of forgiveness and restoration to favour, whether human or Divine."

**J. C. Lambert,** "Confession," in A Dictionary of Christ and the Gospels: Aaron–Zion, ed. James Hastings (Edinburgh; New York: T&T Clark; Charles Scribner's Sons, 1906), 360.

# Congregational

"It is of great moment to be fully persuaded, that when we have sinned, there is a reconciliation with God ready and prepared for us:"

**John Calvin and John Owen**, Commentaries on the Catholic Epistles (Bellingham, WA: Logos Bible Software, 2010), 167.

# Interdenominational

"To walk in the light is to live in fellowship with the Father and the Son. Sin interrupts, but confession restores that fellowship. Immediate confession keeps the fellowship unbroken"

**C. I. Scofield,** ed., The Scofield Reference Bible: The Holy Bible Containing the Old and New Testaments (New York; London; Toronto; Melbourne; Bombay: Oxford University Press, 1917), 1321.

"Rather than denying our sinfulness, John advocates that we "confess our sins" (1 John 1:9). This will do much more toward advancing our relationship with God than ignoring our sin, as the separatists advocate."

**William R. Baker and Paul K. Carrier,** James-Jude: Unlocking the Scriptures for You, Standard Bible Studies (Cincinnati, OH: Standard, 1990), 242.

"Knowledge of one's own sinfulness cannot remain a simple act of recognition; it must lead to ὁμολογεῖν, "confession.""

**Georg Strecker and Harold W. Attridge**, The Johannine Letters: A Commentary on 1, 2, and 3 John, Hermeneia—a Critical and Historical Commentary on the Bible (Minneapolis, MN: Fortress Press, 1996), 31–32.


"Confession, he does not speak of sin in general (as a state), but of definite, concrete, specific sins"

**John Peter Lange et** al., A Commentary on the Holy Scriptures: 1, 2, 3 John (Bellingham, WA: Logos Bible Software, 2008), 37.


"...urges his readers to confess their specific sinful deeds, that is, the evil they are actually doing"

**C. Haas, Marinus de Jonge, and J. L. Swellengrebel**, A Handbook on the Letters of John, UBS Handbook Series (New York: United Bible Societies, 1994), 30.


"The sinner is to believe (John 3:16). The saint is to confess. The word confess" is homologeō (ὁμολογεω), from homos (ὁμος), "the same," and legō (λεγω), "to say," thus, "to say the same thing as another," or, "to agree with another." Confession of sin on the part of the saint means therefore to say the same thing that God does about that sin, to agree with God as to all the implication of that sin as it relates to the Christian who commits it and to a holy God against whom it is committed. That includes the saint's hatred of that sin"

> **Kenneth S. Wuest**, Wuest's Word Studies from the Greek New Testament: For the English Reader, vol. 13 (Grand Rapids: Eerdmans, 1997), 104.

"It is important here to notice the plural, sins, which implies a detailed and specific confession of our wrong thoughts, words, actions and attitudes. It includes the good which we omit, as well as the evil which we do."

> **David Jackman**, The Message of John's Letters: Living in the Love of God, The Bible Speaks Today (Leicester, England; Downer's Grove, IL: InterVarsity Press, 1988), 38.

"In view of verse 8, Christians ought to be ready at all times to acknowledge any failure which God's light may expose to them. Thus John wrote, If we confess our sins, He is faithful and just and will forgive us our sins and purify us from all unrighteousness."

> **Zane C. Hodges**, "1 John," in The Bible Knowledge Commentary: An Exposition of the Scriptures, ed. J. F. Walvoord and R. B. Zuck, vol. 2 (Wheaton, IL: Victor Books, 1985), 885.

"Confessing sins is not 'saying you're sorry.' It is agreeing with God that a particular act is sin—and thus taking sides with Him and against yourself."

**Lawrence O. Richards**, The Bible Reader's Companion, electronic ed. (Wheaton: Victor Books, 1991), 892.

"For believers to confess sin is to admit the continual need of Christ's cleansing blood"

**Robert B. Hughes and J. Carl Laney**, Tyndale Concise Bible Commentary, The Tyndale Reference Library (Wheaton, IL: Tyndale House Publishers, 2001), 708.

"Confessing our sins does not mean a shallow reciting of misdeeds. It means owning up to wrongdoing and bringing our lives into line with God's goodness and commands."

**Robert W. Yarbrough**, "1 John," in CSB Study Bible: Notes, ed. Edwin A. Blum and Trevin Wax (Nashville, TN: Holman Bible Publishers, 2017), 1994.

# Lutheran

"The confession of sins must correspond to 'walking in the light'"

**Rudolf Karl Bultmann**, The Johannine Epistles a Commentary on the Johannine Epistles, Hermeneia—a Critical and Historical Commentary on the Bible (Philadelphia: Fortress Press, 1973), 21.

"There are two kinds of sin: one kind is confessed, and this no one should leave unforgiven; the other kind is defended, and this no one can forgive, for it refuses either to be counted as sin or to accept forgiveness"

**John Stott**, The Preacher's Notebook: The Collected Quotes, Illustrations, and Prayers of John Stott, ed. Mark Meynell (Bellingham, WA: Lexham Press, 2018).

"This is what 'doing the truth' when 'the truth is in us' means: we shall ever confess our sins, admit, acknowledge them to God"

**R. C. H. Lenski**, The Interpretation of the Epistles of St. Peter, St. John and St. Jude (Minneapolis, MN: Augsburg Publishing House, 1966), 392.

"The Greek verb translated forgive suggests that forgiveness is conditioned on the confession of sin, and is a singular act rather than a general state."
**Robert Kysar**, I, II, III John, Augsburg Commentary on the New Testament (Minneapolis, MN: Augsburg Publishing House, 1986), 40.

"What are to be confessed are αἱ ἁμαρτίαι ἡμῶν, i.e. the sins of Christians, which are the particular manifestations of ἁμαρτίαν ἔχειν (so also Braune); therefore the plural."
**Joh. Ed. Huther**, Critical and Exegetical Handbook to the General Epistles of James and John, trans. Paton J. Gloag and Clarke H. Irwin, Critical and Exegetical Commentary on the New Testament (Edinburgh: T&T Clark, 1882), 292–293.

"...so that John not only says, that if we have sinned we must confess; but that all have reason to say, I have sin,"
**Johann Albrecht Bengel**, Gnomon of the New Testament, ed. M. Ernest Bengel and J. C. F. Steudel, trans. William Fletcher, vol. 5 (Edinburgh: T&T Clark, 1866), 114.

"After 1520 Luther held that confession of sins was still "obligatory" and that "secret confession" to another

Christian, although not required by Scripture, was 'useful and even necessary.'"

**Walter A. Elwell and Barry J. Beitzel**, "Confession," in Baker Encyclopedia of the Bible (Grand Rapids, MI: Baker Book House, 1988), 506.

# Methodist

"And if sin is committed it needs confession."
**Arno C. Gaebelein**, The Annotated Bible, Volume 9: James to Revelation (Bellingham, WA: Logos Research Systems, Inc., 2009), 137.

"The plural "we" belongs to the debating style of the letter, but may also indicate a public, corporate context for such confession"
**Judith M. Lieu**, I, II & III John: A Commentary, ed. C. Clifton Black, M. Eugene Boring, and John T. Carroll, 1st ed., The New Testament Library (Louisville, KY: Westminster John Knox Press, 2012), 58.

"What he does say is that if we confess our sins (1:9), or agree with God about our need, that engages a God who is both faithful and just. He will both forgive us our sins and purify us from all unrighteousness. The writer is making the case that the inner tendency to sin and the practice of sinning are realities and need to be faced and admitted.

Then God will respond with His transforming goodness to give us forgiveness and freedom."

**David A. Case and David W. Holdren**, 1-2 Peter, 1-3 John, Jude: A Commentary for Bible Students (Indianapolis, IN: Wesleyan Publishing House, 2006), 232.

# Patristics

"John has combined the fact that we should entreat God for our sins and that we should obtain mercy when we do so (Cyprian of Carthage)"
**Gerald Bray,** ed., James, 1-2 Peter, 1-3 John, Jude, Ancient Christian Commentary on Scripture (Downers Grove, IL: InterVarsity Press, 2000), 172.

"If we acknowledge our sin and confess it, he will forgive it, and not only that one but all our sins."
**Andres**

"Since we cannot live in this world without sin, the first hope we have of salvation is through confession"
**Bede the Venerable**

"Further, whoever is not conscious of sin, either is not guilty of sin, or has forgotten his sin. If, therefore, mortal sins are forgiven by a general confession, whoever is not conscious of a mortal sin, can be certain that he is free from mortal sin, whenever he makes a general confession:"

**Thomas Aquinas**, Summa Theologica, trans. Fathers of the English Dominican Province, vol. 9 (London: Burns Oates & Washbourne, n.d.), 569.


"For the baptized who have deserted or violated the faith, forgiveness may be obtained through the heartfelt repentance exhibited in uttering a confession of sin, doing genuine penance and living good lives afterwards"

**Augustine, John R. Franke**, ed., Old Testament IV: Joshua, Judges, Ruth, 1–2 Samuel, Ancient Christian Commentary on Scripture (Downers Grove, IL: InterVarsity Press, 2005), 362.

# Pentecostal

"It is true that God has provided pardon for all the believer's sins on the ground of the all-sufficing atoning blood of Christ, but what God has thus provided we appropriate to ourselves by confession of sin and prayer for pardon"

    **R. A. Torrey**, What the Bible Teaches: A Thorough and Comprehensive Study of What the Bible Has to Say Concerning the Great Doctrines of Which It Treats (New York, Chicago: Fleming H. Revell Company, 1898), 435.

"Christ breaks sin's grip; you are no longer in bondage to it. However, since Christians are not made perfect, they still find the need to ask Christ for forgiveness when they sin. First John 1:9 has been called "the Christian's bar of soap": 'If we confess our sins, He is faithful and just to forgive us our sins and to cleanse us from all unrighteousness.'" Assemblies of God (**Ken Horn**, Sin and Salvation https://news.ag.org/en/article-repository/news/2019/11/sin-and-salvation#:~:text=However,%20since%20Christians%20are%20not,cleanse%20us%20from%20all%20unrighteousness.")

"And somehow I feel that we who have been denying the power of the cross in our preaching ought to go back to the places where we have thus put our Master's sacrifice to an open shame, confess our sin, and promise there to be faithful in lifting up 'the Lamb of God that taketh away the sin of the world.'"

**Chas. A. Bowen**, Chapter XVIII: A Message from Missions to the Modern Ministry, vol. 3 (Bellingham, WA: Logos Bible Software, 2005), 257.

"There is an emphasis on the importance of confessing one's sins to maintain fellowship with God, highlighting that this act is not about a single moment of repentance but rather a continuous process of acknowledging sin and seeking forgiveness as we walk in the light of God's truth; it's a key aspect of living a Christian life in genuine communion with God."

**Gordon Fee**, 1 John 1:9

"The Church of God has affirmed the importance of repentance and confession. We tell unbelievers to confess their sins so that God will forgive them. However, the Bible teaches us that repentance is also needed in the Church and in the lives of individual Christians. In the New Testament, the call to repentance is addressed to the unbeliever (see Acts 17:30), to the Jew (see Acts 2:38), and to the Christian alike (seeRevelation 2:5)."

**Lee Roy Martin** (ThD) to the Church of God Doctrine and Polity Committee on Friday, April 11, 2019. R.H. Also see: Gause, Cheryl Bridges Johns, Lee Roy Martin, John Christopher Thomas, and A.J. Tomlinson,

"If we do one thing: confess our sins, God will do four things:
1. Be faithful to us.
2. Be just with us.
3. Forgive our sins.
4. Cleanse us from all unrighteousness."

**Finis Jennings Dake**, The Dake Annotated Reference Bible (Dake Publishing, 1997), 1 Jn 1:9.

"…often repentance is more broadly defined to include actual change in character and behavior, but Scripture describes this as the 'fruit of repentance' (Matt. 3:8) or 'deeds consistent with repentance' (Acts 26:20; cf. Matt. 7:16; Luke 3:9; 8:15; John 12:24; Rom. 7:4; Gal. 5:22; Col. 1:10)" (pp. 119)."

**Michael Horton**, The Gospel-Driven Life

# Presbyterians

"Penitent confession and acknowledgment of sin are the believer's business, and the means of his deliverance from his guilt."
    **Matthew Henry,** Matthew Henry's Commentary on the Whole Bible: Complete and Unabridged in One Volume (Peabody: Hendrickson, 1994), 2443.


"...confess—with the lips, speaking from a contrite heart; involving also confession to our fellow men of offenses committed against them."
    **Robert Jamieson, A. R. Fausset, and David Brown**, Commentary Critical and Explanatory on the Whole Bible, vol. 2 (Oak Harbor, WA: Logos Research Systems, Inc., 1997), 526.


"Sins. Note the plural, as compared with the singular, sin, in the previous verse. See note. The plural indicates that the confession is to be specific as well as general. Augustine's words are exactly to the point, but his play upon pardon and confess cannot be reproduced in English."

**Marvin Richardson Vincent**, Word Studies in the New Testament, vol. 2 (New York: Charles Scribner's Sons, 1887), 321.

"Pardon in the Scriptures, always supposes that there is confession, and there is no promise that it will be imparted unless a full acknowledgment has been made."

**Albert Barnes**, Notes on the New Testament: James to Jude, ed. Robert Frew (London: Blackie & Son, 1884–1885), 285.

"God has promised that he will never despise the contrite heart and he will not break his word. If we humbly and sorrowfully confess our sins, he will forgive."

**William Barclay**, The Letters of John and Jude, 3rd ed., The New Daily Study Bible (Louisville, KY; London: Westminster John Knox Press, 2002), 37.

## About the Author

Dr. Mark Spitsbergen is the Senior Pastor of the Abiding Place in San Diego, California where he and his wife Anne have pastored since 1985. He holds a Bachelor of Arts Degree (BA) in Biology/Chemistry from Point Loma Nazarene University, a Master of Science (MS) from the University of Saint Andrews, a Doctorate of Theology (ThD) from School of Bible Theology, as well as a Doctorate of Ministry (D. Min.) from Life Christian University. He has been studying Biblical languages since 1983. He began his study of biblical languages at PLNU and also studied at UCSD with Dr. David Noel Freedman.

www.ingramcontent.com/pod-product-compliance
Lightning Source LLC
LaVergne TN
LVHW041337080426
835512LV00006B/501